SOUTH

FESTIVITIES

SOUTH INDIAN FESTIVITIES

P.V. JAGADISA AYYAR

Rupa & Co

© P.V. Jagadisa Ayyar

First in Rupa Paperback 1998
First impression 1998

Published by
Rupa & Co.
15 Bankim Chatterjee Street, Calcutta 700 073
135 South Malaka, Allahabad 211 001
P.G. Solanki Path, Lamington Road, Bombay 400 007
7/16, Ansari Road, Daryaganj, New Delhi 110 002

ISBN 81-7167-373-2

Typeset by
Megatechnics
19A, Ansari Road,
New Delhi 110002

Printed in India by
Gopsons Papers Ltd.
A-28, Sector-IX,
Noida - 201 301

Rs. 95

CONTENTS

APPENDICES

Author's Introduction

It is but a truism when we say that the life of an orthodox Hindu consists in the observance of a large number of fasts and festivities. The origin and rationale of most of these are lost in obscurity with the passage of time. The traditional explanations, found scattered in certain rare manuscripts, proverbs, sayings, and even in some of the nursery rhymes of the Hindus, have been lost; and in the course of time, are sure to be completely beyond the reach of humanity if immediate steps are not taken to gather and preserve them.

It is proverbial that the Hindus follow the customs of their forefathers blindly, without understanding in the least the real motives behind their origin and the basic principles underlying them. Though many stories may be narrated to illustrate this fact, I will briefly narrate only one and then go on.

Once upon a time a great sage performed a sacrifice. A large number of people assembled to witness the event. A tame black cat was seen tied to the pillar supporting the sacrificial shed with a rope of *kuśa* grass (*Eragrotis cynosuroides*). This was done to prevent it from coming there and upsetting the sacrificial vessels and arrangements. However this was interpreted by the simple-minded audience to be a sine qua non for the observance of such a sacrifice. From that time onward, great pains were taken by the performers of that sacrifice to secure a black cat! An act aimed at geting rid of a nuisance turned into an act of primary importance in the performance of the sacrifice, simply because the people did not care to know 'the why and the wherefore' of particular acts.

Every village has a temple, and people circumambulate it. Ask them why it should be done and you are taken for an impertinent unbeliever.

The use of turmeric powder with lime water, to cast off the influence of evil eye, is a common sight during marriage occasions and marriage processions; but how many will be able to give a rational explanation for the usage?

We may quote instances after instances of people following a particular custom blindly, without understanding why and wherefore they do it. Such a practice is surely not conducive to general welfare.

The Hindu festivals and *Vratas* were designed by the great sages of old. They were full of wisdom and capable of understanding and utilising the forces of nature. They thoroughly understood the human nature and human wants. They also knew about the dangers from super-physical forces and intelligences that humanity is susceptible to. Just as flypapers are used to get rid of flies, substances like a mixture of turmeric and quicklime in a quantity of water were used, to get rid of super-physical pests, directing super-physical forces that are injurious to human safety and welfare. They originated temples, festivals, Vratas, fasts and so forth with definite aims. As they were thoroughly conversant with the needs of men while living, and also with their needs after they died, their aims may be said to be twofold. For convenience's sake, we may sharply divide their aims into physical and spiritual. The festivals, Vratas, fasts, and other such activities are designed to serve either or both of these aims.

From the standpoint of those wise sages, physical acts are for serving spiritual ends, and consequently people who take a short cut to spiritual progress need not attach much importance to observances fostering physical gifts, but may utilise them as temporary stepping stones to reach greater heights. But a very large majority cannot take this short cut at this stage of human evolution, and consequently the observance of the festivals and Vratas should naturally be of a kind conducive to bodily comfort and relief, contributing but little to spiritual progress. But each and every one of the festivals and Vratas has a deep spiritual significance, and persons capable of taking the short cut to spiritual progress may advance very rapidly, if they understand the principle underlying the observance, and take to it in the right manner and in the right spirit.

If physical results are to be taken into consideration, there are myths attached to each and every one of the fasts, feasts, Vratas and festivals, and if people understand them and follow in the footsteps of the heroes depicted therein, physical results are sure to follow sooner or later.

When spiritual progress by the observance of a particular Vrata is to be explained, we must examine what takes place in nature everyday around us, and see whether there may not be anything akin to it, in the birth, growth, decay, and death of man. We should also see that our sacred scriptures are used as touchstones for testing our inferences.

Everyone will concede that there is a goal towards which everything in nature is tending. The aim of a tree is to produce seeds capable of reproducing the parent tree. The same thing applies to the animal kingdom also. Herein lies the key to unravel the mystery of the nature and progress of human spirit. Only this fact is emphasised by the phallic symbol in Śiva temples and the images of gods and goddesses in all temples.

The human body and the human principles are but layers within which the seed, namely, the spirit, is forming and maturing or ripening. When the seed is fully ripe, it will have no use whatsoever for the human body and the human principles and consequently it would shake or cast them off and begin to grow to acquire the shape and size of the parent it originated from. Let us take the formation and growth of this spiritual seed for our examination. To do this satisfactorily and clearly, we must distinctly bear in mind the simile of the seed. The principle out of which the tree grows is in the kernel we all know. This kernel has layers of pulp, skin and so on to protect it until it is capable of resisting extraneous influences. Human spirit is exactly like this kernel imbedded in layers of matter going by the name *kośas* or sheaths in Hindu philosophical parlance. Unlike the layers in a seed, the layers surrounding and protecting the spirit are cast off and renewed in the same way in which the slough of a serpent is cast off and renewed.

Scientists tell us that there are invisible forces between atoms and molecules holding them together. By stretching our imagination we can conceive these lines of forces gradually developing into minerals and vegetables. In fact, these are the lines on which the future nervous systems of animals are to be developed. The Hindus consider certain trees and plants in the vegetable kingdom, and certain animals in the animal kingdom, to be more evolved than the others. This conception is the result of observations made on the development of these lines of forces.

These lines of forces, after reaching a particular stage of development, manifest themselves as fine streaks of light emitting a halo around them. These streaks, by play of forces, gather around them material sheaths of various grades of tenuity, forming the complicated nervous systems of animals. The various ganglionic knots are centres of brilliance gathering around them material sheaths similar to the nervous sheaths. These centres of brilliance with the network of fibres of light diffusing a halo of light forming a definite beautiful shape within an ovoid of light, is really the spirit of man.

Brighter these centres and streaks of light in animals are, finer will be their nervous systems and consequently better bodies for receiving finer vibrations of emotion and intellect, built around them. The development of these centres and the connecting network of streaks of light to the point of perfection, is, in fact, the goal towards which human and other evolutions are tending. The Hindu philosophy and its system of Yoga are intended mainly to achieve this end. When this point of evolution is reached, the kośas or material sheaths having served their purposes, would fall off from the spirit to which they are now clinging, leaving it free to complete its own growth in the likeness of its parent.

Just as there are differences in the seeds in the number of the protective coverings for the kernels, there are differences in the intelligences also in the universe. The intelligence having the largest number of coverings, goes by the name 'man,' and those having fewer ones, go by the names of various grades of angels or *devas*. There are hosts of them and they are of innumerable kinds and varieties. But the kernel or the spiritual principle in every one of them is the same.

The sages of old knew this, and consequently originated a variety of festivals with the progress of the spirit in view. For the progress of the spirit, the well-being of the various coverings is absolutely necessary till it is completely developed. Therefore the various customs and observances are so designed as to lead to spiritual growth, first by strengthening the coverings, and eventually but gradually, by throwing off those coverings, when they have accomplished their purposes.

Men in different stages of attainment or evolution are found in this world. Some require the outermost sheath to be strengthened for the welfare of the spirit within; to them, the observances would secure a healthy and strong body.

Some may require good emotional coats, and others, mental coverings. The proper observances of the festivals would give to each, what he or she wants for the evolution of spirit in him or her.

The Hindu temples are intended to show by concrete physical designs the constitution of man both in his higher and lower aspects. The various *prakaras* stand for the various protective coverings, the deity in the sanctum sanctorum or the innermost *sabhā* or hall of the temple stands for the human spirit.

When the spirit gets tired of the outermost coating, it casts it away and uses the next one, to be cast away after a while, repeating the process with each and every one of the coverings, till it stands in its own effulgence. The attainment of this stage is the Hindu conception of *Mukti* or liberation from birth and death.

From what is set forth above, it will be clear that the aims of the observance of the Hindu festivals appear contradictory; some contributing to the welfare of the body at the expense of the spirit and some to the welfare of the spirit at the expense of the body or sheaths in man. There is also a maxim, 'Live in body and die in spirit and live in spirit but die in body.' In fact, if one cares for spiritual progress he should cast off material attachments, since such attachments result in birth and death, detrimental to the growth of the spirit.

In the early stages, the spirit grows with the growth of the body — physical, emotional and mental. Finer these bodies are, by regulated and selected matter, emotion, food, and thought supplied to build them, more and more beautiful will be the radiant spirit and the colours emitted by it with every passing emotion and thought.

It is very interesting to note that only a few selected temples, rivers, localities and mountains, are considered potent enough to bestow the maximum benefits on men. The reason is that the progress of humanity as a whole is overseen by some special intelligences recognised as Adhikarika Purushas or souls entrusted with the authority, by higher and mightier entities. They magnetise special centres and consequently, progress in those localities will be easier to achieve. Further, forces are liberated and poured on this earth on particular occasions. For bestowing maximum benefit on humanity, it is essential that a large number of people assemble at a selected place on a particular occasion favourable for the purpose. This aim is achieved by magnetising certain centres to draw people there in large numbers in order to benefit them. Hence have arisen famous religious localities, temples, rivers, and hills.

The festivals described in this volume will be found to have been originated to propitiate one or the other of the Hindu Trinity — Brahmā, Vishṇu and Rudra. Temples dedicated to Brahmā and festivals observed to propitiate him will be found to be very few, and, in fact, we may say they are nil and negligible. The reason for this is obvious. Brahmā's duty is to create and we are all created. So there is no need to propitiate him. We see struggle for existence everywhere. Everyone tries hard to preserve his life and possessions and consequently the propitiation of the preservative aspect — Vishṇu — is the most essential thing. Hence the worship of Vishṇu and the devas like Indra, Yama, and so on, who are in a way under him, is the prominent feature in all religious observances meant for the preservation of body, health, wealth and so on.

Emotional elevation and progress is the next important thing. The emotional aspect is like a hinge. It has two halves, so to say, one attached to the material world and the material body and its needs, and the other to intellectual achievements.

To serve the first purpose, episodes in the lives of saints like Nanda, are enacted in a manner to stir the emotions latent in men, and thereby help the spirit to polish one of its facets, or in other words, to develop one of its aspects. With this object in view, certain great Hindu teachers had started the devotional schools called *Bhajan* parties. The great *bhaktas* (mystics) like Kabir referred to at length in books like 'Bhakta Vijayam' exemplifying the devotional aspect.

Next comes the sphere of intellectual progress which has given rise to several schools of philosophy.

The attainment of the goal is possible through what is called Mysticism or *bhakti* for some. Such people should take to the observance of such festivals or Vratas that could serve their purpose.

The goal may be reached through intellect also. Men capable of taking to this path, should observe the Vratas dedicated to deities like Subrahmanya and Vināyaka who symbolise wisdom.

The shortest but the most difficult and dangerous path to reach the goal is said to be the path of *yoga*. It is said to be as short and narrow as the razor's edge. People capable of taking to this path may observe the Vratas dedicated to Śiva, the destructive aspect.

There are also Vratas observed to propitiate the devas. These could confer on men boons only within their limited jurisdiction. For the attainment of the final goal, observance of festivals and Vratas dedicated to one or the other of the Trinity, namely, Brahmā, Vishnu and Śiva, is highly essential. In Hindu Scriptures, we find ancient sages performing penance invoking the presence of one of the Trinity only and not the devas like Indra, Kubera, and so on.

In conclusion, I may say that people should first of all try to understand their place and temperament in the ladder of evolution, and take to the systematic observance of a selected Vrata, throughout their lifetime to attain the desired end. Though they may observe all the festivals and Vratas, each one of them should have a special Vrata, so that the deity presiding over it may be drawn to them and bestow on them the desired end. At any rate, all people should try to understand the reason behind the observance, before taking to a specific Vrata. Then and then only will this land of spirituality, India, with the help of cumulative influence of spiritual progress in the land, will regain its lost, or at any rate, almost completely disappearing, prestige. When this stage is re-attained, the condition of the Krita age will be restored. With the ardent desire to initiate mental exertion in this direction, this volume is launched into the world by its author and dedicated to the sages — the Adhikarika Purushas. May their blessings rest on humanity!

I   Bhogi Pandigai

Of the many Hindu festivals, the one going by the name 'Bhogi Pandigai,' is observed on the last day of Dakshiṇāyana[1] or the period of the sun's southerly course. The day is also the one, which precedes Makara[2] Sankrānti[3]; the occasion when the sun enters Capricorn. The festival is observed in the month of January in honour of Indra[4] on elephant, the god of the heavens, who is supposed to control the clouds and cause seasonal rains heralding thereby a period of abundance and prosperity in the country. In fact, this festival and the next two, namely, Sankrānti and Go Puja, are similar to the observances of the harvest feast in the countries of Europe. The term 'Bhogi Pandigai' means 'the festival of physical enjoyment.' The name has its origin perhaps in the bringing in of the harvest which is the source of all enjoyment. The *ryots* have then their well-earned rest after a period of strenuous exertion in the fields.

Moreover, it is the commencement of the Hindu marriage season, and jocose people use to say that 'the marriage court is open.' At any rate the festival is considered to be the harbinger of the coming period of marriages and enjoyment, and is consequently observed by the people in a fitting manner.

A good deal of scrubbing and cleaning goes on in all the houses in the country. Prior to daybreak on the festive day, the dirt and rubbish accumulated throughout the year are swept out and burnt. The whole village presents a smart and tidy look. As the northerly course of the sun then commences, the six months beginning from that date, go by the name of 'Uttarāyana' and the particular occasion itself is

called 'Uttarāyana Punyakalam,' i.e., 'the auspicious hour
when the sun commences its northerly course, entering the
Capricorn.'

There is also a very interesting myth attached to the
festival. In the Dwāpara Yuga[5], Lord Sri Krishna[6] desired to
teach Indra a lesson since he was found to be rather arrogant.
So he prevailed upon the Yādavas (shepherds) of Brindavana[7]
to offer sacrifices to the Govardhana[8] mountain instead of to
Indra, on the Bhogi Pandigai day of a particular year, stating
that they were not agriculturists to care for the seasonal rains
of Indra, but were cowherds depending on the Govardhana
mountain, which afforded rich pasturage for their cattle.
When Indra saw that he was balked of his legitimate offerings
by the machinations of Sri Krishna, he grew angry and wanted
to punish the Yādavas for listening to the evil advice of
Krishna. The clouds that bring rain, thunder and lightning are
said to be seven in number and they were under Indra's orders.
Induced by their master, the seven clouds began to rain very
heavily in the territory of the Yadavas, who, terrified at the
severity of the supernatural rain that was falling incessantly
for days together destroying men and cattle by thousands,
hastened to Sri Krishna and solicited his help.

Krishna thereupon lifted up the Govardhana mountain by
his occult powers and held it aloft. The Yādavas with their
cattle and other belongings took shelter under the lifted-up
mountain, till Indra ordered the clouds to desist, finding
himself thwarted in the attempt at browbeating the Yādavas.

Eventually, Indra recognised Lord Vishnu in Sri Krishna
and began to repent his folly, in having tried his prowess
against that of one of the Trinity.

Sri Krishna also relented and permitted the Yādavas to
resume the old custom of celebrating the Bhogi Pandigai in
honour of Indra.

There is a strong belief among the Hindus, that a really pious man should not die during the months of Dakshiṇāyana, but should die only during Uttarāyana. Some even go to the extent of saying that only those people who die during Uttarāyana go to heaven, while those who die during Dakshiṇāyana remain in the various levels of the nether world, till they are born again in the world to work out their karma (action, from Sanskrit *kru* = to do) by playing the part assigned to them in the world's drama of life.

Anyhow, the months falling in the period of Dakshiṇāyana are generally unhealthy, bringing in their wake, disease and death, while those in the Uttarāyana bring to the people, vitality and health. The sun is said to nourish not only our earth, but also the various planets and stars comprised in his system. The planets specialising the vitality absorbed by them from the sun, pour it in our world to be used by men, animals and plants. As most of the stars and planets are in the north, and very few in the south, the southerly course of the sun is detrimental to their absorption of vitality from it, and consequently there is a reduced receipt of specialised vitality flowing from the various planets and stars. This is perhaps the main reason for the people welcoming with delight the advent of Uttarāyana. In this connection, the Hindu custom of burning a corpse with the head placed towards the south may be noted, since it shows that the southern direction is symbolical of death, and in fact, Yama, the god of death, is said to reside in that direction. The story of Triśanku hurled down from the heavens by Indra but suspended in the south by Viśwāmitra by his prowess and who is said to be shining there even now as 'the southern cross' bears out the statement made above when rightly pondered over.

In Mahabalipuram near Madras, there is a sculptural[9] representation of the scene relating to the Govardhanagiri incident described in the myth[10] quoted above. From the incident of Krishna lifting up the mountain and saving the people of Brindavana, his aspect here is known as Govardhana Uddhāra Krishna. The *mandapa* or portico in which this incident is sculptured goes by the name of Krishna mandapa.

NOTES

1 A course (from Sanskrit ay = to go). sun's progress from one solstice to another. Uttarāyana or northward progress, from 'Tai' to 'Ani' and Dakshināyana or southward progress, from 'Adi' to 'Margali' are the two ayanas which compose a year. The former is the day and the latter the night of the devas (celestials). It is during the latter that everything done, though virtuous in itself, is considered unprofitable in effects; while those done in the former are supposed to have a virtuous effect. Consequently all Hindus devote themselves to the study of the Vedas, celebration of marriages and auspicious rites during the Uttarāyana period.

2 Means 'dolphin' as the sun stands in that zodiacal constellation.

3 The passage of the sun from any one sign into another. In common usage specially applied to Makara Sankrānti.

4 For detailed information consult *South Indian Shrines* by P.V. Jagadisa Ayyar.

5 This and other *Yugas* are dealt with in *South Indian Shrines* by P.V. Jagadisa Ayyar. There are four Yugas, the first of which is Sat or Krita, then follow Tretā, Dvāpara, and Kali. The anniversary of the first day of the Sat Yuga falls on the third lunar day in the bright fortnight of Vaiṣākha (April-May); the four incarnations in this age were the Matsya or fish, Kurma or tortoise, Vārāha or boar, and Nrisimha or the man-lion. The anniversary of the first day of the Tretā Yuga falls on the ninth lunar day in the bright half of Kārtika (October-November); the incarnations in this age were the Vāmana or Dwarf, Parasurama

and Rama. The anniversary of the first day of the Dvāpara Yuga falls on the thirteenth of the waning moon in the month of Bhādra (August-September) of which Sri Krishṇa and Buddha were the incarnations. The anniversary of the first day of the Kaliyuga is the full moon day in Māgha. Kalki will be the incarnation in this age. On all these anniversary days a bath in some sacred river and charity are enjoined. On these days water mixed with sesame seeds should be regularly presented to the progenitors of mankind (Pitris.) Fig. 1. on page 84 of An Alphabetical List of the *Feasts & Holidays of the Hindus and Muhammadans,* Superintendent, Government Printing, India, 1914.

6 Is said to correspond to Apollo of the western mythology.

7 See also *South Indian Shrines* by P.V. Jagadisa Ayyar.

8 For further information reference may be made in *South Indian Shrines* by P.V. Jagadisa Ayyar.

9 This is illustrated in *South Indian Shrines* by P.V. Jagadisa Ayyar.

10 Detailed version can be had from Wilson's translation of *Vishṇu Purāna.*

II   Sankrānti

T he name Sankrānti is a general one given to the day on
which the sun passes from one sign of the Zodiac[1] (rāsi)
to another; yet it has a restricted application and special
reference to the day on which the sun enters the house
called Makara (Capricornus) in the Tamil month of Tai
corresponding to the English months of January-February.
The occasion is called 'Makara Sankrānti[2]' though the Tamil-
speaking people call it 'Pongal[3] Pandigai' for the reason that
the newly harvested rice is first cooked and this preparation
goes by the name *pongal*.

It is laid down in the Hindu scriptures that food should be
cooked not with the object of eating but only to serve the
purpose of a sacrifice and an offering to God[4]. The remnant
of the food, if any, after the sacrifice, may be eaten. Hence
the newly harvested rice is cooked as an offering to the sun
whose vitality, going by the different names of electricity,
magnetism, and so forth, nourishes everything in the world,
both in the vegetable and animal kingdoms.

Though the sun is worshipped primarily and chiefly on this
occasion, yet the other elements favouring the increase of the
flock and the produce of the crops are not ignored. Vāyu, the
god of wind, is worshipped on the occasion, since he is the
lord of the monsoons without which no rain is possible. The
tutelary deity of the family called the 'Griha Devatā' is also
worshipped to ensure a happy life in the house, and the
worship goes by the name of 'Vāstu Puja'[5].

An open courtyard is a sine qua non in all houses of a
South Indian village, to perform marriages in, for exposing

grain and other things to the sun for drying, and so on. In this courtyard a spot where the bright sunlight falls is chosen for the performance of the puja. The place is well scrubbed, cleaned and washed with cowdung mixed with water. A lotus patera with octagonal petals is designed with powdered rice deftly scattered by the ladies of the house with their forefingers and thumbs. The centre of this is graced with the design of the Sun god, with his consorts Samjā and Chāyā, the former the daughter of the divine architect Viśwakarmā, and the latter her exact replica. The interesting myth relating to the two consorts of the sun is as follows:

Samjā, unable to endure the effulgence of her lord, the sun, went into the forest to perform penance with a view to obtain sufficient strength to withstand the same, leaving her Chāyā (shadow) in her place. The sun, however, came to know of the change effected by Samjā, and consequently went in quest of her. On the way, he found a beautiful mare and immediately fell in love with it. Metamorphosing himself into a horse he had union with that mare and the two Aświns of the Hindu mythology were the fruits of this union, and they are said to be the foremost physicians of the universe.

The children - a son and a daughter - born of Samjā are - Yama, the god of death, and Yamuna, the goddess of the river of that name.

The consort Chāyā, too, had issues born to her, and they were a son and a daughter. The former is the planet Saturn, and the latter is the river Tapti.

When Samjā went to perform *tapas* (penance), she left her two children Yama and Yamuna with Chāyā, the co-wife of the sun, with the request that they might be taken care of, and treated with kindness. Chāyā did treat them with kindness until her own children were born, after which she began to ill-treat Samjā's children.

Yama would not brook the partiality shown by Chāyā to her children and the injustice done to him and his sister. Consequently he kicked his stepmother with his foot in anger, who thereupon cursed him, saying that the foot raised to kick her should become a mass of rotten flesh infested with loathsome worms. Yama then approached his father and represented to him the injustice and unfair treatment meted out to him and his sister by Chāyā and the curse levelled at him by her when he kicked her in protest.

As curses from parents could not be easily undone, the sun mitigated the evil by countermanding the curse and reducing the result to that of worms falling down with bits of flesh instead of permanently infesting the flesh in the foot and giving trouble.

As Yama always espoused the cause of justice and was found to be highly impartial in dealing with one and all, he won the name of 'Dharma Raja,' the king of justice, and was appointed to hold sway over the realms of the dead, where he administers justice without any partiality. No one who commits a sin can escape his punishment, and the punishment inflicted is, in each case, very just.

The myth is said to be a profound allegory containing deep spiritual truth just as the allegory of 'sin and death' in Milton's *Paradise Lost.* In fact, almost all the Hindu myths are allegories. One should pierce through the veil of words to understand the real significance conveyed in the myths.

A bath[6] in certain sacred rivers such as the Cauvery on the auspicious and sacred occasion of 'Makara Sankramana Punyakalam' is considered highly meritorious. People therefore flock in large numbers on this occasion every year at Tiruvadi near Tanjore, considered specially important by the ancient Hindus, as well as in the river Tamparaparni and in the sea at Vedaranyam. A sage named Hemarishi is said to have prayed to Vishṇu on the banks of the tank called 'Pottamarai Kulam' meaning the tank of gold lotuses, in the Sri Sarangapani temple at Kumbakonam on one such auspicious occasion and was blessed with the sight of the lord of the temple, Sarangapani, in response to his prayers. Further the god Sundareśwara of Madurai is said to have performed a miracle, appearing as a magician (*siddhar*) before the multitude and making a stone image of an elephant eat sugarcanes, on a particular Sankrānti day!

There is a stone inscription[7] in the south of the vimānam of the Virarāgava temple at Tiruvallur near Madras. It relates to the granting of land by Chola king Kulottunga for Makara Sankramana festival, in the fifth year of his reign.

NOTES

1 Refer also *South Indian Shrines* by P.V. Jagadisa Ayyar and *Indian Architecture* by A.V.T. Ayyar & Sons, 1920 page 64, Book 1.

2 Makara is supposed to be an aquatic animal of the crocodile species that has now become extinct. The name *mriga* (deer) is supposed to have been made use of to denote this animal; as according to some textual version, Uttarāyana and Dakshiṇāyana are spoken of as the 'deer Sankrānti' and the 'crab Sankrānti' respectively.

3 The name 'pongal' is given to rice boiled in milk. It is generally cooked in the courtyard of the house. The Tamil word '*pongu*' and Telugu one '*pongodhi*' mean 'to boil'.

4 Lord Śiva is said to be highly pleased by the burnt offering on Sankrānti day, of *tila* (sesame) mixed with or soaked in ghee and consequently bestows prosperity on the observers of this Vrata which is given the name of Maha Tila Deepa Vrata.

There is also another Vrata observed on the Makara Sankrānti day to please Śiva and it goes by the name 'Mahavarthi Vrata'.

When the sun enters the Makara rasi, a lamp filled with cow's ghee is burnt using a stout wick of cotton thread.

Some people fast for a month consuming only a very small quantity of milk and that too only when there is the fear of death from hunger and exhaustion. This observance is called the observance of 'Māsa Upavāsa Vrata' and it may commence from the first or the eleventh day of either of the lunar fortnight or from the new moon or full moon day, or from the day on which the sun passes from one zodiacal sign to another. Though the minimum period for the observance of the Vrata is one month, yet it may be continued for three, six or even twelve months, subsisting on milk only when there is the fear of loss of life from complete starvation.

The burning of two sacred lamps on the Sankranti day, one fed with oil and the other with ghee, is believed to have the power to enable the observer of this Vrata going by the name 'Sankaranti-Vrata-Deepodhyapanum', to reach Śiva's or Vishṇu's region after death, according as he worships the former or the latter.

5   The puja called 'Vāstu Puja' is observed when a new house is entered and occupied. It is a ceremony prescribed in the Vedas and the other religious scriptures. No house is said to be fit for human use unless and until this puja is performed in it. If one is desirous to live happily in a house, it is necessary for him to perform this pooja, 'Vāstu' is the presiding deity of the house and he is held in great veneration by the people in India. Hence this puja is to satisfy the presiding deity of the house.

6   "There is not a river in the world which has influenced humanity or contributed to the growth of material civilization or of social ethics to such an extent as the Ganges. The wealth of India has been concentrated on its valley, and beneath the shade of trees whose roots have been nourished by its waters, the profoundest doctrines of moral philosophy have been conceived to be promulgated afar for the guidance of the world." — Imperial Gazetteer, Vol, 1, p. 26, Fig. 2 on page 31 of *Hindu and*

Muhammadan Festivals, John Murdoch, 1904. The devas are always working for the prosperity of human beings. The six months commencing from the Makara Sankrānti day are said to be the daytime of the devas. The morning hours are said to be specially favourable for receiving the influences liberated by the devas for the benefit of humanity. Hence bath and *Japam* (prayer) in the mornings of the days of these six months are ordained in the scriptures of the Hindus.

7 This forms number 1193 on page 466, Volume I, *Manual of the Administration of the Madras Presidency*, Vol.III published by the Government of Madras, 1893.

III Go Puja (Cow Worship)

The day next to Sankrānti is set apart for the worship of cows. The festival is given the name of 'Mattu Pongal' from the custom of cooking pongal for the cows to feed on. Cattle form the chief asset of an agriculturist and consequently it is but proper that their services are recognised. Hence a small portion of the annual produce is utilised to feed them. This is perhaps the simplest explanation that can be given for the origin of the custom.

There is an Indian proverb which says that the joys of the world do not exist where there is no wealth, and cattle formed the wealth of the primitive people. Hence the wise sages of old have laid down that the worship of the bulls and cows at least once in a year is necessary if one wishes to be free from want, disease and sin.

People do worship the sacred animal, the cow, once in a year, not only because the same is enjoined in the scriptures for having good progeny, but also for the fact that its milk forms a very important part of our food, and consequently, it deserves to be specially treated at least once in a year.

The ethical code of the highly evolved of the Hindu sages is quite different from what is in vogue at the present time among ordinary people. The present moral code does not prevent the owner of a cow from sending it to the knacker's yard as soon as it is dry. The owner of a horse or a dog shoots his animal with impunity if it is no longer useful, forgetting the benefit he had derived from it when it was strong and active. But the ancient sages thought that the milk of the cow was meant for the calf, and consequently if a man took the same by force he became a thief. Similarly, they thought that if an animal was useful to an individual even for a very short period,it must be treated with kindness till its death. A man who did not do so, committed the sin of ingratitude. People even go to the extent of saying that the ancient sages never used to kill animals while performing sacrifices, but simply asked them for particular portions of flesh from their body which the latter willingly relinquished. The sages, by their yogic[1] powers, made it possible for the animals to live till the portions given were formed once again in course of time. The same procedure was observed with regard to the vegetable kingdom also by the wise men of old. They recited certain incantations addressing the presiding deity of the plants whose portions they might desire for their use. The deity gladly placed at their disposal the parts solicited. In fact, when sage Kaṇva wanted presents for his adopted daughter Śakuntalā, he got them only in this manner, from the various trees of the forest in which his hermitage was located.

Considering these facts, it is no wonder that the Hindus try to show their gratitude by performing puja of the cattle that were of immense use to them during the past year.

There is a very interesting myth relating to the origin of the cow. As soon as men came into existence, they realised the waste of tissues in their body and felt the need of doing something about it. They naturally approached Brahmā[2] for help. He thought that the celestial nectar would be too strong for men to digest, and consequently took a quantity of it himself, specialised it in his body and reduced it to a form in which men could safely take it.

He then took the form of a cow and made the nectar flow from her udders to feed his children — the human beings. Hence the cow is considered both father and mother and consequently one becomes a patricide, a matricide, and the slayer of Brahmā if he kills a cow. If one ill-treats a cow, he becomes a great sinner. If one worships a cow, he worships Brahmā as well as his parents. If he protects a cow, he protects his parents in their old age.

There is also a sort of sacredness attached to the foam emanating from the mouth of a cow, and the mythical reason for the same is given below.

As soon as Brahmā swallowed a small quantity of nectar and assumed the form of the cow, a large quantity of foam was formed in his mouth and it began to fall on a Śivalingam. As the foam was nothing else but nectar Śiva[3] was highly pleased. From that time onward it was ordained that the foam in the mouth of a cow should be considered as sacred as nectar itself. The sin of pollution attaches itself to the foam in the mouth of any other animal, but in the mouth of a cow it is to be considered holy, and consequently it is as free from pollution as fire, wind, and gold are said to be. In fact, every part of the cow is said to be divine in its origin and it is enjoined in the Hindu sacred scriptures that it should be treated with reverence.

There is yet another myth emphasising the importance of the cow. A Brahmin in the city of Mathura had once owned a cow named Bahula. It was grazing on the banks of the river Yamuna, on the fourteenth day of the bright fortnight of Bhādrapada, that is, in the months of September-October. Suddenly a tiger appeared there and desired to eat the cow.

The cow had a calf whom she loved very much. It, therefore, begged the tiger to permit it to go home, feed the calf and then come back, to be devoured by it. The tiger consented and the cow went home. While the cow was away, the tiger departed its life from an accident that had happened to it. The spirit that was in the tiger's body was in reality a great soul that had accumulated great merit in the past lives and consequently on being liberated from the fleshy tabernacle of the tiger's body, was able to understand the 'why' of things, vouchsafed only to great souls. When the cow returned to the place to become a prey to the tiger, it bade the cow to go back to its calf safe and sound. At the same time, it vouchsafed increase in cattle to one who gifted a cow to another on that particular day in Bhādrapada.

The places considered specially auspicious for the performance of Go Puja are Tiruvamathur near Villupuram, a junction on the South Indian Railway, Karur, in the Trichinopoly district and Avur and Pattisvaram in the Tanjore district.

NOTES

1. *Yogam* (from San. Yuj = to join).

2. Brahmā (from San., Brih = to increase) masculine gender. The first member of the Trimurti. The supreme spirit manifested as the active creator of the universe.

3. Śiva, the god of generation and justice, is represented as riding a bull, which symbolises reproductive energy. His own colour as well as that of the bull is white, referring probably to the unsullied purity of justice. His throat is dark blue, he has matted hair, has three eyes, one being in the centre of the forehead. These are said to note his view of the three divisions of time - past, present and future. His trident is the emblem which shows he combines the attributes of creator, destroyer and regenerator in himself. A crescent on his forehead indicates the measure of Time by the phases of the moon. He is covered with serpents which are the emblems of immortality, while a necklace of human skulls marks the lapse and revolution of ages and the extinction and succession of generations of mankind.

Śiva is the great destroying and dissolving power. But destruction implies reproduction, because the Hindu believes in the transmigration of souls. So as Śiva and Śankara 'the auspicious', he is the reproductive power which is perpetually restoring that which has been dissolved. As a restorer he is represented by his symbol the *lingam* or phallus, typical of reproduction; and it is under this form alone or combined with the *yoni* or female organ, the representative of his *śakti* or female energy, that he is everywhere worshipped. The lingam therefore represents 'life out of death or life everlasting.' 'The spirit of the (lingam) worship is as little influenced by the character of the type as can well be imagined. It is all spiritual and mystical'— H.H. Wilson: Fig. 1 on pp. 75 & 76 of *Hindu and Mahammadan Festivals* , John Murdoch, 1904.

Ratha Saptami

The Hindu festival going by the name 'Ratha Saptami' is observed on the seventh day of the bright fortnight in the month of Māgha, also called Tai Masam in Tamil. It corresponds to the English months of January-February when the sun is in the Makara. The festival is known by different names. Some call it 'Māgha Saptami' deriving the name from the month in which it is considered auspicious. The word 'Saptami' is derived from the Sanskrit word *sapta* which means seven, and consequently, the expression 'Māgha Saptami' means the seventh *tithi*[1] or day after the 'Purṇimā'[2] (full moon) or the 'Amāvasyā'[3] (new moon) in the month of Māgha. Here it is the seventh day in the bright fortnight in the said month. Some people call it Jayanti Saptami and others Mahā Saptami. The expression Jayanti Saptami means the victorious seventh day after the full moon day and that going by the name 'Mahā Saptami' means 'the great seventh day' in the fortnight. The name 'Jaya Saptami' originated perhaps from the belief that the observance of this festival brought success in all undertakings and the name, Mahā Saptami, from the importance attached to this Saptami for being the most auspicious of all the Saptamis falling in the year.

People who subscribe to the heliocentric system, make the Helios or the sun the power station from which force, vitality, etc., are disbursed to the whole solar system. The sun rules the planets, which, in their turn, rule the destinies of men. Consequently the worship of the sun on this occasion is supposed to favourably influence the planets. So a large majority of people worship the sun on this occasion and the temple dedicated to the sun at Suryanarkoil near Tiruvadamarudhur in the Tanjore district in southern India is perhaps the solitary instance of the kind.

Just as the images of a bull and Brahminy kite are made to grace a Śiva and a Vishṇu temple respectively, figures of horses are made to grace the gopuram and the altar-front of a temple dedicated to the sun.

A bull is the vehicle of Śiva and a Brahminy kite is the vehicle of Vishṇu. Similarly, the vehicle of the sun is said to be a chariot drawn by seven horses of rainbow hues.

The sun and the planet Jupiter of the Navagrahas or nine planets are made to occupy the *garbhagriha* or the womb in the body of the temple; while the seven planets are located in separate shrines around the courtyard of the temple. From the plan of construction of the temple and the rarity of such temples in the land, one is led to think that the cosmic conception and the conception of the influence radiating from the sun to the planets and the living beings on the earth, were considered by the sages of old, to be beyond the comprehension of ordinary men.

We may call the rays radiating from the sun 'unit rays.' Each of these unit rays has within it the possibility of the seven coloured rays of the spectrum.

The bundles of rays emanating from the sun are absorbed by the cosmic centres, the planets, and are then radiated back on earth, as bundles of different coloured rays, each planet contributing one variety of colour. All forms in this world have centres in the subtle web of tenuous matter surrounding and interpenetrating them. The rays from the planets pass through all or some of these centres and converge diffusing a halo of light around the form more or less bright, setting in relief the most prominent colour ray reflected by the form.

The combination of rays of different colours in an infinite variety of ways has caused the conception of diversity in forms. This highly philosophical conception is presented in the construction of the sun temple.

This particular day is considered to be the first day of Vaivaswatha Manu who is said to be the first descendant of Vivaswan the sun, as his name implies. Manu is said to be responsible for the evolution of souls in this solar system.

The peculiar custom of people placing a layer of the leaves of the plant *Erukku* *(Calotropis Gigantea)* on the head and bathing with that in rivers, deserves examination. It is believed that this plant symbolises decay. There is a saying that the houses of a partial judge and a false witness are destined to be overgrown with this plant, and its flowers are said to be the favourite flowers of Śiva, the lord of destruction and of the burning ghats. Why should people place some of the leaves of this plant of such evil repute on their heads and bathe on this occasion? The rationale is simple when properly understood. The nature of plants as well as animals is ever undergoing changes with the change of influence of the planets over the objects on earth. A careful observer might notice this in men, animals and plants. In the pharmacopoeia of medical drugs of the Hindu physicians, it is laid down that the drugs would be efficacious only when they are gathered on particular days, at particular hours of the night or the day. The indigo dye in the indigo plant is supposed to remain in the leaves only during particular fortnights and the farmers would not cut the plants unless it is the favourable fortnight. Similarly a chameleon has miraculous magical properties in its tail on Sundays, and people cut it on those days, dry it in the sun, enclose it in a cylinder formed of gold leaf and hang it round a child's neck to ward off the evil influences of spirits and other such entities.

With such beliefs in the background, it is no wonder that people consider the leaves of Erukku to possess miraculous properties on the occasion, and so make use of them while bathing, as explained above.

As the sun burns out everything physical, slowly but surely by his heat, light, electricity and magnetism, so Śiva burns out the desires like lust, anger, envy, malice and so forth. The planets are said to be responsible for the desires in men, and they are most potent during the six months of the sun's southerly course called Dakshiṇāyana. As this particular festival day happens to be the beginning of the sun's northerly course, the energies of the planets are perhaps paralysed for the nonce, thus making it possible for men to feel the nature of the unit ray of the sun, which would, on other occasions, be possible only by the steady shutting out of the influences of the planets from entering and influencing men, by using tremendous will power, not possible in the case of ordinary men. The leaves of Erukku, placed on the head while bathing, symbolise the burning or the washing away of all sins, such as evil desires in man.

It is also laid down in the scriptures that the Ratha Saptami day is specially auspicious, if it happens to fall on a Sunday or when the moon enters the asterism 'Rohini' (*Tauri*). Further, the worship of Gouri, Śiva's consort, by imagining her to be seated on an elephant, at the time when the sun enters the asterism Hasta (*Corvi*), is believed to confer special benefits on the worshipper, such as freedom from sickness and sorrow, and immunity from premature death.

Light is knowledge and the sun as the source of light is the source of all knowledge. In the beginning, there was only darkness and consequently there was no knowledge and the *jivas* too were plunged in darkness or ignorance. Then the mighty being, Iśwara is said to have created the sun to enlighten the world, on a particular day which is being ever afterwards celebrated as the Ratha Saptami day.

In a place called Gangaikondacholapuram in the Trichinopoly district, the planets are represented in a monolithic car having at their top a lotus representing the sun.

The deities presiding over the planets are said to have worshipped Śiva visible to the mortal world as the sun, at Tiruththengoor in the Tanjore district and at Tiruvallum near Madras (now, Chennai).

The worship of the sun on all mornings in the month of Māgha, commencing either from the beginning of the month or from the seventh day of its bright fortnight, is known as Nitya Danya Vrata.

A handful of rice is set apart every day and the accumulated quantity is distributed among the poor at the end of the month.

There is yet another Vrata which is observed to secure lasting youth and it is known as Bala Nithya Vrata. It consists of an offering of six oblations of handfuls of water every morning followed by six prostrations to the sun.

People also observe another vrata called Danapala Vrata commencing from the last Sunday of the bright fortnight of this month to secure immunity from poverty and want.

"There[5] was a city in which there lived a poor Brahmin. He used to go to the jungle to collect *durva*[6] (*Cynodon dactylon*) grass and the twigs of certain trees for fagots to ignite his sacred fire for worship. He once met some fairies who were engaged in worship. He asked them to explain to him the nature of the puja. They said that on the first Sunday of the month of Śravana (July-August) one should arise from bed without speaking a word, should bathe with one's night-clothes on, should bring water without placing the pot on the floor, should draw the figure of the sun on a betel leaf with red sandalwood paste, should draw a whorl with six volutions, should take a twine formed of six threads, should tie six knots in that twine, should offer betel leaves and flowers to the symbol, and worship it. Finally a married Brahmin woman should be fed with dainties and offered clothes or cash. The Brahmin performed the puja in this manner. The sun was pleased with him. He became rich. The queen of the realm sent for him. The poor Brahmin was terrified, he shivered. The queen assured him that there was no ground for fear. He was asked to give his daughters in marriage to the prince and to the son of the prime minister. So he did. The Brahmin retired to his seclusion after the marriage. After twelve years, he came to the city to see his daughters. He first went to the eldest daughter, who herself had become the queen in course of time. She offered him light refreshments, but he could not partake of them because he had to perform the puja of the sun and recite the story. The queen said that she had no time to waste as her husband, the king, was about to start on a *shikar*[7] expedition. The Brahmin, therefore, left the palace, and went to the second daughter. She received him well. She heard his sacred story, she worshipped the sun as advised, and she prospered. Later on, the king left his shikar but lost his way. The queen became very poor — she lost all that she had. She had four sons. On a certain Sunday, in the month of Śravana, her son was sent to her prosperous sister to obtain some help. His aunt received him well and gave him a calabash[8] fruit full of gold coins and jewels. On his way home he met the sun dressed as a gardener, who forcibly took the fruit away. He returned home disappointed. On the second Sunday, the ex-queen sent her second son to her sister. She received him well, and gave him a hollow stick filled with gold coins and jewels. The sun, dressed as a cowherd, met him on his way home, and forcibly took the stick away. On the third Sunday the third son was deputed. He got a hollowed-out coconut filled with gems. He was told not to part with the nut until he reached home, but he placed it on the parapet of a well in order to draw water, as he was excessively thirsty through the influence of the sun. The nut rolled down into the well. On the fourth Sunday, the fourth son got some food from his aunt, but the sun swooped down in the form of a kite and took it away. On the Sunday following, the poor queen went herself to her opulent sister. She also was well received but the younger sister explained to her the folly of neglecting the puja of the sun and allowing their father to leave home without listening to the sacred story. She expressed her regret and began worshipping the great luminary as advised. The sun was pleased and fortune smiled on her again. The lost king returned home safely. She started for her old capital after thanking her younger sister. At the first day's halt she performed the puja and asked her attendants to get someone to listen to her story. A poor dealer in fagots was taken to her. He said he had no time to listen to stories as he had to earn his bread. She took out six pearls, gave him three, and held the other three in her hand while she was reciting the story. The result was that his fagots were turned into gold! He promised to perform the puja and left. At the second stage, a gardener whose well had dried up was brought to the queen. She offered him three pearls and made him listen to her tale with the result that the well was flooded with water and the garden became fertile. At the third stage, an unhappy old woman was brought to her. She gave her three pearls to induce her to listen to the story and showed her how to perform the puja. The result was that her sons, one of whom had been drowned, another who was swallowed by a boa-snake, and the third who had lost his way in a forest, all returned alive. She became prosperous. At the fourth stage, a man who had lost his limbs was placed before her. She placed three pearls on his chest, held the other three in her hand, and recited the tale. The maimed man recovered his limbs! At the fifth stage she reached home. She became happy and always performed the puja with devotion."

NOTES

1   Tithi is the time occupied by the moon in increasing its distance from the sun by 12 degrees; in other words, at the exact point of time, when the moon (whose apparent motion is much faster than that of the sun), moving eastwards from the sun after the Amāvasyā, leaving the sun behind by 12 degrees. *Indian Calendar* , Sewell & Balakrishna Dikhit, 1896.

2   Purṇimā is the time of full moon, or that period of time when the moon is farthest from the sun.

3   Amāvasyā (literally the 'dwelling together' of the sun and moon) is the period of new moon, or that point of time when the longitudes of the sun and moon are equal.

4   Sanskrit *arka* means sun from cuneiform shape of leaf, smooth on the upper surface, clothed with wooly down on the underside, flowering all year. The juice mixed with *uppu* (common salt) is given in toothache; the juice of the young buds is given in earache; the leaves warmed and moistened with oil are applied as a dry fomentation in abdominal pains. Pages 1032 and 1033 of *Manual of the Administration of the Madras Presidency*. Vol.III, the Government of Madras, 1893.

This is a large shrub, common all over India; it is commonly to be found in waste ground among rubbish, ruins, and such like places; flowers, rose colour and purple mixed. (There is a white variety also to which great religious importance is attached). Of late this plant has attracted much attention for the many useful and important purposes which it can serve. An acrid milky juice flows from every part of the shrub when wounded; and this the natives apply medicinal purposes in many different ways, besides preparations of the plant itself in epilepsy, paralysis, bites of poisonous animals, as a vermifuge, etc. In almost all cutaneous affections, especially in leprosy, it is frequently employed, and much attention has lately been bestowed upon its virtues in the cure of the latter dreadful complaint. The root, bark, and inspissated juice are used as powerful alteratives and purgatives. Its activity is said to be owing to a principle called Mudarine, discovered by the late Doctor Duncan of Edinburgh, which he found to possess the singular property of congealing by heat and becoming again fluid on exposure to cold. The root is used in the manufacture of gun-powder charcoal. Page 120 *A Hand Book of the Trees*, Shrubs and Herbaceous Plants, Higginbotham & Co., 1866.

5   Pages 1 to 4, *Hindu Holidays and Ceremonials*, Gupte, Thacker, Spink & Co., 1919.

6   The belief is that it possesses the virtue of purifying everything. See also footnote on page 27, *An Alphabetical List of the Feasts & Holidays of the Hindus and Muhammadans*, published by the Superintendent, Goveornment Printing, India, 1914.

7   Chase, game or hunting expedition.

8   Kushmand (Cucurbita maxima).

V   Tai Pusam

The Hindu festival called 'Tai Pusam,' is observed on the day over which the asterism Pushya (*cancri*) presides, in the Tamil month of Tai which corresponds to the English months of January-February. The day generally falls on the full moon day of the month. The planet Brihaspati or Guru (Jupiter) is said to be the presiding deity of the asterism Pushya and consequently worship offered to the asterism Pushya is considered to have special merit, since Brihaspati symbolises wisdom and the Hindus consider him to be the preceptor of the gods, and one of the most important of the nine planets. A bath in a secred river on this day is considered to be very meritorious and people, both men and women, young and old, flock to the nearest one for the purpose.

The place called Tiruvidaimarudur in the Tanjore district is one of those important places where this festival is celebrated. There is also a myth regarding the way in which of this festival originated there, and it is as follows:

It is said that before the commencement of the present iron age of Kaliyuga, and at the close of the silver one of Dvāpara, there lived a king in the Chola kingdom by name Hamsa Dvajan (the king with the flag having a swan embroidered on it).

Blessed with a religious bent of mind, he thought of going on a pilgrimage to different sacred places such as Benares, Gaya and so forth, but his onerous duties as a king prevented him from undertaking the journey.

Learning from the Hindu Śāstras, expounded by wise sages, that if he deputed a pious Brahmin to make the tour in his place it would win for him the same merit which he could earn if he went on pilgrimage himself. Therefore, he secured the services of a Brahmin, promising him a handsome reward in return. He further promised that he would take care of the Brahmin's family during his absence.

The Brahmin set out on an auspicious hour with good wishes from one and all, and the king, true to his promise, took care of Brahmin's family.

Time passed on and nothing noteworthy happened, till at last one night, the king, while on a nightly peregrination to glean information about his administration, came close to the Brahmin's house. Wishing to know what was happening inside, he peeped through the window. To his susprise and anger, he saw the Brahmin's wife in the amorous embraces of someone. He thought this man to be her lover, not realising that it might be her husband who had returned.

As a representative of the Brahmin, the king had to do what the Brahmin would have done under the similar circumstances. In a fit of jealousy, the Brahmin would have killed the Brahmani and her lover. As the lady in question was left in the king's charge during the Brahmin's absence, he must deliver her safe and sound to her husband, leaving the question of punishment to the husband himself. But the lover should not escape the punishment. Thus argued the king to himself, and rushing inside the house with his drawn sword he stabbed the poor Brahmin who fell down without a groan and expired.

Discovering but too late the mistake committed by him in hot haste, the king shed copious tears of repentance and tried to console the widow. Do what he would, the sin of having caused the death of a Brahmin who had gone on a pilgrimage for him, would not leave the king. The spirit of the deceased Brahmin haunted him constantly. He wandered hither and thither, unable to shake himself free from the incessantly haunting spirit, and at last met a sage named Bhargava and sought his advice. Advised by him to visit various sacred places, he went on a pilgrimage and came at last to Tiruvidaimarudur. Having bathed in the sacred water of the well called Sidha-Tirtha inside the temple, he began to enter the temple itself. When he crossed the second entrance of the temple, he found that he was free from the spirit that was haunting him till then! The king was much pleased with the result. As he was freed from the haunting spirit on the Tai Pusam day, the king made large gifts to the temple for the annual celebration of this festival.

There is yet another myth to emphasise the importance of Tiruvidaimarudur as a sacred place for the observance of the Tai Pusam festival and it is as follows:

Once upon a time, there ruled in Madurai a king named Varaguna Pandyan. While riding one day, he caused the death of an aged Brahmin unwittingly, riding over him and trampling him under his horse's feet. He became the murderer of a Brahmin and a great sinner in consequence. He was further possessed by the spirit of the deceased. He wanted not only to be freed from the sin but also to be rid of the ever bothering spirit of the Brahmin whom he had unwittingly killed. Even the sacred place Madurai could not effect this. He tried many other sacred places also, but his efforts did not bear fruit.

One night he had a dream in which Sri Sundareśa, the presiding deity of the Madurai temple, appeared before him and wanted him to visit the temple at Tiruvidaimarudur to be freed from his troubles. But that place was in the Chola kingdom, and the king Pandyan did not like the idea of entering the territory of another king soliciting his favour. While he was at a loss to know what to do, god Sundareśa, the patron of the Pandyan line of kings, came to his rescue. He told him that the king of the Chola country would invade his territory, but would only meet with defeat at his hands, and flee back to his country being hotly pursued by him, and then that occasion would give him an opportunity to enter the temple at Tiruvidaimarudur.

Everything transpired as Sri Sundareśa had foretold in the dream. The Pandyan king did enter the temple at Tiruvidaimarudur. When he passed through the second entrance of the temple, the spirit[1] of the Brahmin possessing him did not dare to follow him and consequently was left behind.

Finding immense relief, and fearing that the spirit left behind might take hold of him again if he returned by the way he went in, the king made his exit through a back entrance to the west of the temple, and reached a place called Tribhuvanam that was close by. From that place he made arrangements for the annual celebration of the Tai Pusam festival at Tiruvidaimarudur endowing the temple with gifts, since his liberation from the haunting spirit was also effected on the Tai Pusam day.

From the above narratives it will be seen that the temple at Tiruvidaimarudur is considered highly sacred by the Hindus. There is a *bael* tree[2] in the temple and people circumambulate it to obtain success in their undertakings. One Vasuman, a king of the Vidhehas (Behar), is said to have regained the kingdom he had lost, by circumambulating this particular tree.

A bath in the river Tamparaparni at Tinnevelly[3] on the Tai Pusam day is considered highly meritorious for the reason that Iśwara had blessed Iśwari who was doing penance there on its banks, on the Tai Pusam day.

It is also laid down that Indra, the king of the celestial regions, got rid of his sin on the Tai Pusam day at Tiruppudaimarthur in the Ambasamudram taluk of the Tinnevelly district and consequently, the observance of Tai Pusam festival there is highly meritorious.

Lord Subrahmanya, the second son of Iśwara, is worshipped at Vaithiswarankoil[4] as Mutthukumara, on account of his lovely form as a fine youth. His weapon is a lance called *velayutham* and it is said to be an invincible one bestowed on him by Parvati on the Tai Pusam day. Hence people observe this festival at Vaithiswarankoil also, considering the place specially auspicious for the purpose.

The next place where this festival of Tai Pusam is observed is Palni,[5] the famous centre of pilgrimage in southern India. It is dedicated to Subrahmanya, the second son of Śiva and Parvati and is visited every year by thousands of pilgrims of all castes and shades of religious opinion.

There is an inscription[6] on the southern wall of the central shrine in the Mahalingaswami temple at Tiruvidaimarudur, Tanjore district, which refers to a gift of land on this festival day.

There is a record[7] on the base of the western wall of the Vedapurisvara temple at Tiruvedikudi, Tanjore district, which relates to a grant of 13 *velis* of land for this Pushya festival.

There is an inscription[8] on the eastern wall of the second *prakara* in the Panchanadesvara temple at Tiruvadi, Tanjore district, which relates to the time of king Bukka II, Saka 1303, Durmati, making a gift of 19 velis of land for this festival.

NOTES

1 See also *South Indian Shrines* by P.V. Jagadisa Ayyar.
2 Bael or bel tree is specially sacred to Śiva. It is of middling size, armed with sharp spines. A decoction of the root, leaves and bark is a remedy in several diseases. The mucus of the seed is a good cement for some purposes. It grows all over India, commonly about the temples and all other sacred spots like flower garden, river banks etc.

As a rule the leaves consist of 3 leaflets and they often grow in clusters of 2 or 3 on what appear to be arrested branchlets, pages 105 & 106,*Some Madras Trees* by Butterworth, 1911.

3   This place is fully described in Chapter XXXI of *South Indian Shrines* by P.V. Jagadisa Ayyar.

4   This place is fully described in Chapter VIII of *South Indian Shrines* by P.V. Jagadisa Ayyar.

5   This place is fully described in Chapter XXVIII of *South Indian Shrines* by P.V. Jagadisa Ayyar.

6   This is numbered as 248 of 1907 : *Madras Epigraphical Department*, (No. 275, page 1270, Volume II, *Inscriptions of the Madras Presidency*, published by the Government of Madras)

7   *Inscriptions of the Madras Presidency*, published by the Government of Madras, No. 1464 E.,/on page 1425, Volume II.

8   *Inscriptions of the Madras Presidency*, published by the Government of Madras, No. 1505 E., on page 1428, Volume II.

VI

Masi Māgha

Masi Māgha is a festival observed by the Hindus in the month of Māgha, also called Masi in Tamil, corresponding to the English months of February-March, on a day when the asterism Māgha (*Leonis*) holds sway. The day of observance of this festival will generally be the full moon day of the month Māgha referred to above. The deity presiding over the Māgha asterism is said to be Brihaspati (Jupiter), considered by the people to be the preceptor of the gods also. Hence offering worship to him on this festive occasion is believed to confer on people all the desired boons, if it is done in the right way and in the right spirit.

In all the temples of the land, festivals in honour of the presiding deities are celebrated, and people flock to those temples in very large numbers not only to witness the observance of the festival but also to take active part in the same.

There is a mythical statement that Iśwara had his initiation at the hands of Sri Subrahmanya in Swamimalai[1] near Kumbakonam in the Tanjore district on this particular festive occasion. The famous place under reference is situated on the north bank of the river Cauvery and the sacred temple itself is located on a little hillock.

The goddess of the universe is said to have appeared at one time on this earth of ours, being born as a daughter to a king named Daksha Prajapati, in the form of a *śankha* (conch-shell), right turned (*Turbenella Pyrum*), considered by the people to be rare, sacred, and capable of bestowing on its owner immense prosperity. The king Daksha is said to have found the beautiful conch on a lotus flower in the holy spot called Kalindi near Allahabad on the river Jamna, a tributary of the holy river Ganges of the Hindus. When he tried to handle the precious find, it turned into a fine and attractive female child and it was forthwith handed over to his queen to be taken care of and brought up as their own child! The divine gift of this child in such a miraculous manner is said to have taken place on a Masi Māgha day and consequently the occasion has derived its special importance.

The place considered as the most sacred and important for the observance of this festival in southern India is the Mahā Māgha tank in the town Kumbakonam[2]. There are nine rivers in India which are considered by the people to be most sacred and they are, Ganga (Ganges), Jamna (Yamuna), Godavari, Saraswati, Narmada, Cauvery, Kumari, Payoshni and Sarayu. The waters of all these holy rivers are said to be present in the Mahā Māgha tank at Kumbakonam on this festive occasion. Consequently people from all parts of India flock here to bathe in the sacred tank and get purified of their sins.

The above named rivers are also worshipped as sculptures placed in the temple of god Viśvanatha at the northern bank of the Mahā Māgha tank itself.

The tank is said to have been in bad need of repairs prior to the regime of Govindappa Dikshithar, the prime minister of the Nayak kings of Tanjore. During his time, however, the tank was properly repaired, and as many as sixteen temples were constructed on its banks.

Though gifts are given by one individual to another or to a large number of people or in support of charitable institutions, yet this practice has unique modes of observance. Of the many ways of helping people by gifts, the one called *tulabhara*[3] is worth noticing. This mode of gift consists in weighing oneself against gold and distributing the precious metal to the deserving poor. At times, the gold so weighed, is utilised for building or renovating temples or for opening charitable institutions.

One of the Nayak kings of Tanjore is said to have adopted this mode of gift to repair the Mahā Māgha temple at Kumbakonam and to build temples on its banks. He weighed himself against gold coins and with the amount he not only repaired the tank but he also caused the erection of temples on its banks.

There is also a sculptural representation of this tulabhara incident of the Tanjore Nayak king, on the bank of the Mahā Māgha temple at Kumbakonam, which confirms the facts narrated above.

Besides the sacred centres mentioned above, a bath in Sethu near Rameswaram[4] where the two seas Rethnakara (Indian Ocean) and Mahodhadhi (Bay of Bengal) join, or in Vedaranyam,[5] is considered to be of great importance. The river Swarnamukhi at Kalahasti[6] is also considered a sacred one and a bath in it on the occasion of the Mahā Māgha festival is said to bestow a special merit.

Though the asterism 'Māgha' recurs every month, that occurring in the month of Masi is considered specially important. Further the Mahā Māgha festival is celebrated at Kumbakonam once in twelve years and that occasion is considered to be very important. People flock to the place from all parts of the land to bathe in the tank and take part in the festival. The year in which such Mahā Māgha festival is observed, is not considered auspicious for certain purposes. People do not generally perform marriages in that year.

We have epigraphical evidence to show that the famous Vijianagara king Krishnadevaraya witnessed the Mahā Māgha festival. At the entrance into the north gopuram of the Vedanarayanaswami temple at Nagalapuram,[8] Chingleput district, there is a record of this. The king himself dated Saka

1445, *Svabhanu* referring to the visit he paid to Aragandapuram (i.e Nagalapuram) on his way to Kumbakonam to attend the Mahā Māgha festival. An inscription on the north wall of the mandapa in front of the central shrine in the Uttaravedisvara temple at Kuttalam,[9] Tanjore district, refers to the gift made by King Krishnadevaraya on the occasion of the Mamangam festival in Saka 1440, *Dhatri* in favour of the temple of Sonnavararivar. On the west wall of the Ganeśa shrine in the Nedungalanathasvami temple at Tirunedungalam,[10] Trichinopoly district, there is an inscription dated the ninth year of the reign of Chola king Rajarajakesarivarman (985-1013), relating to a gift of land for feeding 550 Sivayogins during the seven days' Masi festival.

NOTES

1 See for further particulars Chapter XII of *South Indian Shrines* by P.V. Jagadisa Ayyar.

2 See for further particulars Chapter XII of *South Indian Shrines* by P.V. Jagadisa Ayyar.

3 For a full description see page 142 of *Archaeological Survey of India* (Annual Reports published by the Government of India) for the year 1912-13.

4 Further particulars are given in Chapter XXX of *South Indian Shrines* by P.V. Jagadisa Ayyar.

5 Further particulars are given in Chapter XXI of *South Indian Shrines* by P.V. Jagadisa Ayyar.

6 Further parpticulars are given in Chapter XXV of *South Indian Shrines*, P.V. Jagadisa Ayyar.

7 In Kotihar, in Kashmir, there is a fountain which, it is said, continues dry for 11 years, and only when the planet Jupiter enters Leo, the water springs out. This position of Jupiter marks

the completion of 12-years cycle of that planet, page 224 *Hindu Holidays and Ceremonials*, Gupte, Thacker, Spink & Co., 1919.

8 This is numbered as 628 of 1904 *Madras Epigraphical Department* (Annual Reports published by the Government of Madras) (No. 700) page 399, Vol. I *Markandeya Purana*, M.N. Dutt, 1897.

9 This is numbered as 493 of 1907 *Madras Epigraphical Department* (Annual Reports published by the Government of Madras) (No. 606) page 1306 Vol, II P.M.P.

10 This is numbered as 687 of 1909 *Madras Epigraphical Department* (Annual Reports published by the Government of Madras) (No. 553) page 1579 Vol. III P.M.P.

VII

Maha Śivarātri

Maha Śivarātri is a Hindu festival observed on the night of the fourteenth day of the dark half in the month of Māgha, called Masi in Tamil, corresponding to the English months of February-March. It is observed in honour of Śiva, one of the Hindu Trinity, representing the destructive aspect in the universe. Though generally, the night time is considered sacred and suitable for the worship of the feminine aspect of the deity, and the daytime for that of the masculine aspect, yet on this particular occasion Śiva is worshipped during the night time, and, as a matter of fact, it is specially enjoined to be observed then. The observance of the Vrata is believed to secure for the devotee immunity from the effects of sin committed either wittingly or unwittingly. The night is divided into four quarters, each quarter going by the name of a *jama*[1] also called *yama*, and pious people keep awake during every one of it, worshipping Iśwara.

It is said that the whole world was destroyed once and the goddess Parvati worshipped her husband Śiva then, and prayed to him that the jivas (living souls) suspended in space like particles of gold dust in a lump of wax during that long period of *pralaya* (deluge) night, should, when they became active once again, have his blessings if they worshipped him just as she did then. Her prayer was granted. The night which Parvati fixed for mortals for the worship of Iśwara was named Maha Śivarātri, or, the great night of Śiva, since pralaya is brought about by him.

There are five kinds of Śivaratris in the course of a year and they go by the names Maha Śivarātri, Yoga Śivarātri,

Nitya Śivarātri, Paksha[2] Śivarātri and Masa Śivarātri. The term Mahā Śivarātri and its origin have already been explained above. Nitya Śivarātri is the daily night of Śiva while Paksha Śivarātri and Masa Śivarātri are Śiva's fortnightly and monthly nights respectively. Yoga Śivarātri is the night which a yogi creates for himself by his yogic trance.

The people who observe this Śivarātri Vrata take only a single meal during the day previous to the Vrata day and sleep in a clean place during the night. In the morning of the Vrata day they take a bath in the waters of a sacred river like the Cauvery, if possible, and then go to witness the divine worship in a Śiva temple, and offer worship to Śiva during every one of the four yamas at night. It is ordained in the scriptures that those who want to observe the Vrata very scrupulously, should worship Śiva with lotus flowers, offer him a preparation called pongal, which is nothing but rice and green dal mixed and cooked together, and then recite the Rig Veda till the first yama is over.

In the second yama, they should worship him with Tulasi[3] leaves (*ocymum sanctum*), offer a kind of preparation called *pāyasam*, a kind of sweet soup-like preparation, and then recite the Yajur Veda till its close.

In the third yama, he should be worshipped with bael leaves *(Aegle marmelos)*, also called Bilvam in Tamil; food mixed with sesame powder should be offered to him and the hymns of Sāma Veda should be recited.

In the fourth or the last quarter of the night, he should be worshipped with blue lotus called Neelothpalam or Sengalinir, should be offered pure and simple food and the Atharva Veda should be recited.

There are myths emphasising the importance of the worship of Śiva during the Śivarātri night and they are as follows:

Once there was a hunter, who went into the forest one day, to procure meat for his family by hunting some animal. He wandered up and down in the forest from morning till night in search of game but was unable to shoot any. At last, when night overtook him, he climbed up a bael tree to escape from a wild animal that was pursuing him. The animal lay down at the foot of the tree quite certain that the man would fall down either from sleep or from exhaustion, and then he would eat him. The hunter, exhausted as he was from his exertions and hunger, wished to scare away the animal by throwing handfuls of bael leaves at it. These leaves dripping with water on account of the recent shower, fell on a Śivalingam that was near. The night happened to be the Mahā Śivarātri night. He had fasted during the whole day since he could not find anything to eat. The drenching rain constituted a bath and his action of throwing the bael leaves on the Śivalingam, the worship of Śiva. Though his actions were not intentional to worship Śiva, yet he is said to have gained heaven as he had observed the Śivarātri Vrata, though unwittingly.

A Brahmin youth of a very bad character was once banished from his country as a punishment for his evil deeds. One day he was wandering from morning till night without anything to eat. After sunset he saw a Śiva temple and entered it. The temple priests had placed offerings before the image of Iśwara. None was there when this youth went inside. Seeing that the coast was clear he thought of walking away with some of the offerings and eating the same elsewhere. As the lamp placed there did not burn brightly, so he trimmed it. But before he could commit theft, he was seized by the priests and put to death. He is said to have reached heaven because he had observed Mahā Śivarātri Vrata since the day in which he fasted happened to be Śivarātri day and his action of trimming the lamp for making it bright, constituted an offering of the food stuff to Iśwara on the Śivarātri night.

The basic principle underlying the observance of the Mahā Śivarātri Vrata appears to be to emphasise the fact that death is sure to follow birth, night is sure to follow day, pralaya to active cosmic life and so on. Consequently while enjoying the one aspect people should always bear in mind its opposite and regulate their life accordingly. They should not be elated at success nor should they allow themselves to be disheartened by failures, but always have trust in God and worship him.

The temples considered specially holy for the worship of Iśwara on Mahā Śivarātri nights are those at Tiruvaikavur near Papanasam in the Tanjore district, Omampuliyur near Vaithisvarankoil in the South Arcot district, Srisailam[4] in the district of Kurnool and Kalahasti in the North Arcot district.

On a pillar in the southern porch of the *mukha mandapa* of the Mallikarjuna temple at Srisailam, Kurnool district, there is an inscription[5] dated Kali 4505 and Saka 1326, Tarana, Śivarātri day. It relates to the incident of gifting that very mandapa by the Vijianagar king Virapratapa Harihara Maharaya II.

On the west wall of the central shrine in the Ratnachalesvara temple at Ratnagiri, Trichinopoly District, there is a record[6] of Chola king Rajaraja III making a gift of 1000 kasus for the expenses incurred on the Śivarātri day.

In the temple of Nagesvaraswami at Vijiamangalam, Coimbatore district, there is a record[7] of Virarajendra (1207-52) making offerings and gifting 90 lamps on the day of Śivarātri in the 14th year of this reign.

On the doorpost of the entrance into the Tambrattiamman temple at Solamadevi, Coimbatore district, there is a record[8] in the 24th year of the reign of Vikrama Chola (1005-45?) which mentions a gift of money for the Śivarātri festival to be observed at the temple of Rajaraja-Isvaram-Udaiyar in Kadappadi *alias* Virasolapuram.

NOTES

1 Jama and yama mean a watch, as measure of time (Sanskrit *yama* = motion). Approximate actual value, I jama or I yama = 1 English hour. This is generally applied to night hours.

2 Paksha (literally a wing) is the moon's fortnight.

3 This is said to be a great purifier of the atmosphere and the destroyer of mosquitoes. See also on *South Indian Shrines* by P.V. Jagadisa Ayyar.

4 This place is fully dealt with in Chapter XXXIX of *South Indian Shrines* by P.V. Jagadisa Ayyar.

5 This is record No. II of 1915 *Madras Epigraphical Department* (Annual Reports published by the Government of Madras) (No. 447 page of 952 Vol. III. *Inscriptions of the Madras Presidency*, Government of Madras, 1919)

6 This is record No. 155 of 1914 *Madras Epigraphical Department* (Annual Reports published by the Government of Madras) (No. 87 page of 1519 Vol. III *Inscriptions of the Madras Presidency*, Government of Madras, 1919)

7 This is record No. 584 of 1905 *Madras Epigraphical Department* (Annual Reports published by the Government of Madras) (No. 236 page of 544 Vol. I. *Inscriptions of the Madras Presidency*, Government of Madras, 1919)

8 This is record No. 242 of 1909 *Madras Epigraphical Department* (Annual Reports published by the Government of Madras) (No. 490 page of 573 Vol. I. *Inscriptions of the Madras Presidency*, Government of Madras, 1919)

VIII   Sri Rama Navami

Sri Rama Navami is the birth anniversary of Sri Rama celebrated by the Hindu devotees in the month of Chaitra (March-April). It falls on the ninth day of the bright fortnight when the asterism Punavasu (*Geminorum*) is in the ascendancy. The observance of this Vrata is said to absolve one from all sins. Men of all grades and ranks observe this Vrata for obtaining prosperity, longevity, happiness and wisdom.

The Lord Mahāvishṇu, one of the Hindu Trinity, representing the preservative aspect of the universe as in his previous incarnations (*avatars*),[1] descended into the world to kill the ten-headed Asura named Ravana who was an epitome of the ten *ahamkaras* (egoism) of men. When one is under the sway of the ahamkaras, his the power of discrimination between right and wrong is destroyed. Consequently the Lord's light has to descend on him to destroy these ahamkaras.

Sri Rama was a brilliant star of the dynasty of Raghu. The history of his glorious reign is a description of his virtues such as faith in God and *guru* (the preceptor), devotion to parents, scrupulous regard for truth, patience in the midst of difficulties and troubles, mercy for the inferior animals, consideration and great regard for different varṇas, fraternal love, regard for elders, popularity among his people, sound and tactful politics, generosity to and forgiveness for, repentant sinners and so on. Every one of the qualities and virtues enumerated above, is proved in his reign.

The famous story of Rama is known as the Ramayana. There is a stereotype proverb current in every house, wherein the women when they sing to make their babies sleep, the burden of the lullaby is — 'The utterance of Sri Rama's name washes away all sins and that of Sita's name kills grief.'

The character of Rama in epic further fulfils the function of a moral preceptor to the world. It awakens in a son, a sense of duty to his parents. It creates in a wife sincere love for her husband. Brothers are roused to the sense of fraternal love and affection. Kings are made to realise the glory of a golden rule. Generally speaking, the benefits said to result from a perusal of this epic with great devotion and reverence for its hero Sri Ramachandra, are as detailed below:

The issueless are said to beget issues. The poor are said to become rich. The forlorn king becomes a king with a large retinue. The imprisoned get released from prison as proved in the story of Ramadas which is being sung throughout the length and breadth of the land in the form of a ballad. Further, it is also laid down that people disgusted with the temporal concerns obtain spiritual bliss from the devotional study of Ramayana.

The epic under reference is divided into six parts going by the names, *Bala Kandam, Ayodhya Kandam, Aranya Kandam, Kishkindha Kandam, Sundara Kandam* and *Yudha Kandam.*

Let us take these parts or *Kandams* one by one and summarise the events detailed therein.

The Bala Kanda — In this, Daśaratha, Rama's father, performs a sacrifice or *Yajna*[2] for obtaining sons making his wives shake off their curse by the merit derived by the said action. Four sons are born to him through his wives. When they reached their youth, the sage Viśvāmitra obtains Daśaratha's consent to take two of his sons Rama and Lakshmaṇa to the forest. On the way, Rama killed an Asura woman, named Tāḍakā. He thereafter bent Śiva's bow and married Sita, daughter of Janaka, the king of Mithila. He subsequently got the better of Paraśurama who challenged him to bend his bow, which feat he accomplished easily and won the same from him. This portion of the epic is intended to throw light on his prowess, love of mankind, hatred for obstinate vice, love for truth and patience in learning archery and other arts of warfare.

The Ayodhya Kanda — This depicts the story how king Daśaratha held a great council and also how he unwittingly killed the son of a *rishi* in a royal hunt. The rishi cursed him that he too should die of grief of separation from his sons. As a result of this curse, Rama, accompanied by Sita and Lakshmaṇa, had to go to the forest abandoning his kingdom being exiled from it by Kaikeyi, one of Daśaratha's queens. There he got acquainted with a king of hunters named Guha, who was the ruler of Sringaberapura. With his assistance, Rama crossed the Ganges in a boat, in company with his brother and wife.

He subsequently reached the mountain called Chitrakoota and dwelt there with his wife and brother having erected a hermitage to live in.

Bharata, in whose favour Rama had relinquished his kingdom of Ayodhya in order to enable his father to keep up his promise to his wife Kaikeyi, returned from his maternal grandfather's house and rebuked his mother for her conduct in having caused the exile of his dearly loved brothers Rama and Lakshmaṇa and his sister-in-law Sita. Daśaratha died of grief in the meantime. Bharata then went in search of his brother in order to request him back to Ayodhya's throne as Daśaratha had wished.

When Rama heard from his brother Bharata about the demise of his dear father, he was grief-stricken and performed his funeral ceremonies as laid down in the Smritis. He then consoled his brother Bharata and sent him back to look after the administration of Ayodhya till he returned. He also gave him his sandals at latter's request, to be placed on the throne, since Bharata insisted that he would only rule as Rama's representative and not as king of Ayodhya.

In this section, his special virtues such as implicit obedience to his father and deep fraternal love combined with great goodness of heart, have been brought out.

The other glorious features depicted with great artistic skill here are, a father's grief at the separation from his dearly loved sons and daughter-in-law which resulted in his death, the fearless devotion a wife who was ready and willing to brave anything to be in the company of her lord whom she deeply loved, the true spirit of a brother in Lakshmana bound to Sri Rama by deep fraternal affection. These are very rare and admirable virtues revealed to the world to be followed.

The Aranya Kanda — In this division of the epic, Sita requests her lord Sri Rama and brother-in-law Lakshmana not to kill *asuras* without sufficient reasons lest sin might result from hasty actions.

Lakshmana disfigures Surpanakha, an asura woman, in order to put an end to her importunities begging Rama and him to marry her. Then the demons Kharadushanas are destroyed by the brothers.

One day, Sita is carried off to Lanka[3] (Ceylon) by Rāvaṇa. Jatāyu, Daśaratha's friend, is mortally wounded by Rāvaṇa, when he tries to rescue Sita from his clutches. Rama, wandering about in search of his lost Sita, discovers the bird Jatāyu who expires after showing him the direction in which Sita was carried off.

Having performed the obsequies of his father's departed friend, Rama proceeds southwards towards Lanka as it was the direction indicated by Jatāyu.

This division is intended to show Sri Rama's love of penance, his great regard for great men and his determination to kill lust and extirpate vice.

The Kishkindha Kanda — In this division Rama's stay at Pampa Saras (Humpi) and the destruction of the monkey chief Bali are graphically described, subsequent to his meeting with Hanuman and the resultant compact of friendship with Sugriva, Bali's brother.

Hanuman is sent in search of the whereabouts of Sita with the signet ring of Sri Rama, to be shown to her in order to convince her of his identity. He is successful in finding her and has a personal conversation with her.

In this part the spirit of devotion with which Hanuman fulfils the functions of a true and trustworthy messenger is depicted. Further, Sita's feeling of intense grief and sorrow, her trust in God and her love for her husband are also described beautifully.

The Sundara Kanda — Herein is narrated the crossing of the ocean by Hanuman, the coming out of the mountain Mainaka from the bosom of the sea to afford a resting place for Hanuman, in return for the help rendered by Hanuman's father, Vāyu, in escaping from Indra who was clipping the wings of mountains, to prevent them from flying from place to place and crushing cities and towns. Then Hanuman enters the island of Lanka and meets Sita Devi in Rāvaṇa's pleasure garden, going by the name 'Aśokavātikā.' He consoles her after having given Rama's signet ring to her and after having taken from her some of her hair ornaments to be shown to Rama.

After having shown to Rāvaṇa that he treated him and his powers with contempt by destroying his favourite resort Aśokavātikā and his capital city Lanka, he returns to Sri Rama, tells him of the discovery of Sita, giving him her hair ornament.

The Yudha Kanda — In this part is described the construction of the bridge to reach the island of Lanka from the mainland, Rama's meeting with Vibhishaṇa, Rāvaṇa's brother, and the compact of friendship with him, and the final destruction of Rāvaṇa and his mighty army of Rakshasas.

Rama then returns to Ayodhya in an aerial vehicle called Pushpaka Vimānam after having placed Vibhishaṇa on the throne of Lanka. He is welcomed there by one and all and crowned the king of Ayodhya amidst great rejoicings.

A perusal of this portion of the epic gives an insight into the military arrangements of the period.

The hero of this epic Sri Ramachandra of the solar line of kings is said to have installed in Rameswaram[4] a Śivalingam as an expiation for the sin committed in having slain a large number of rakshasas in Lanka and elsewhere.

Near the bottom portion of the eastern wall on the west side of two prakaras of the Ranganatha temple at Srirangam[5] is an inscription recording that in Saka 1400 *Manmatha*, Balayyadeva Maharaja gave a village as an offering to god for the celebration of Sri Rama Navami in the reign of Virapratapa Raya. On the north base of the Kothandaramaswami temple at Uragadam,[6] Chingleput district, there is a record relating to the gift of land in *Srimukha, Vaigasi*, on 28th day to Raghunatha Perumal at the same village for conducting the Sri Rama Navami festival.

NOTES

1   The importance of the various avataras of Vishṇu and the shrines dedicated to them are narrated in *South Indian Shrines* by P.V. Jagadisa Ayyar.

2   From Sanskrit *yaj* = to sacrifice, consult page 1027 of *Manual of the Administration of the Madras Presidency.* Vol.III, Government of Madras, 1893.

3   Sanskrit Simhala. Simhala is the name by which it was called by the later Buddhistic writers, being a Sanskrit corruption of

the original and being lion's abode, hence the modern term Singhalese. A descriptive name for Ceylon in some *Purāṇas* is Ratna Dweepam or island of gems. The Sanskrit Lanka, again meaning beautiful, was the old mythological name of Ceylon in the old literature of Buddhism and Brahmanism. Page 153, *Manual of the Administration of the Madras Presidency.* Vol.III, Government of Madras, 1893.

4 This place is fully described in Chapter XXX of *South Indian Shrines* by P.V. Jagadisa Ayyar.

5 This is item No. 491, page 1571, Vol. III of *Inscriptions of the Madras Presidency*, Government of Madras, 1919.

6 This is numbered as 250 of 1913 in the records of the *Madras Epigraphical Department* (Annual Reports published by the Government of Madras) (Page 351, Vol. 1 of *Inscriptions of the Madras Presidency*, Government of Madras, 1919)

Bhagirati Amman
(Kerela).

Thee Chatti
This is a festival of the Amman temples where burning charcoal is held in a pot. Belief goes that the charcoal does not burn the palm as the goddess blesses the individual and also wards off the spirits.

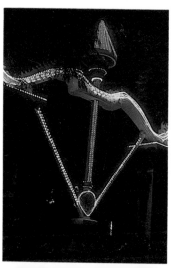

Ooty Flower Festival
Held once every year the entire hill city of Ootacammand emanates with fragrance. The festival is a major attraction as the Queen of Nilgiris abounds with the choicest of flowers and is a major tourist attraction. Competitions are held and flowers and plants from all over the world are displayed. The event is truly a botanist's delight.

Kolam/Rangoli

Kolam is an integral part of South Indian life. Front yards of all houses are washed with gobar (cow dung) and designs are made with fine rice flour.

Various competitions are held during Pongal. Kolam, a marked feature of all festivities in the south, is an art which is taught from one generation to another. In weddings a special type of kolam is used and one can identify the caste of the individual, by the kind used.

Kavadi is a festival of Lord Subramaniya. The devotees carry milk and water and take a vow of celibacy for forty days. They also pierce their body, tongue and other parts of the body with spears.

Traditional dance from
Karnataka.

Arupathy Moovar. This festival is held once a year in Saivite/Shiva
temples. The Nayanmas or those who praise Lord Siva in their songs
are taken on a palki held by men on the four streets surrounding the
temple. Tradition goes that Siva and Parvati, alongwith their
disciples, Nandi, their sons Ganapathi and Karthikeya visit the land
to bless all. The fair goes on for 10 days after Kodiyettan or hoisting
of the flag.

Chithrai Festival. It falls in the first month of the Tamil calender. The whole countryside reverberates with the joy of harvest. The temples have their annual festival to begin with. Community lunches and fairs called chandar are held, (known as Mela in the north and Haat in the east.)
The city of Madurai is famous for this festival.

Pall Kudam. Pall literally means milk. A pot is filled with milk after prayers are held in honour of Amman. The goddess is given a holy abhishek or bath on this occasion.

Purattasi Saturday. This is the sixth month of the Tamil calender. The month is taken as a period of prayer for Lord Venkateshwara. Money, rice and food grains are collected and people walk up to the holy temple of Tirupati. People from all communities and class pray for fulfillment of their wishes. If they attain it the same day they complete by a walk up the mountain with offerings.

Thiagaraja Music Festival. Thiagaraja was a renowned devotee of Lord Rama. His songs are known for their melody and the Pancharatna Kirtanas composed by him is a treatise. The festival is held once a year at Tiruvaiya near Thanjavur on the banks of the Cauvery. Many music connoisseurs, musicians and critics take part in this festival.

Kalakshetra. Founded by Rukmani Devi in idyllic surroundings of the Theosophical society, this place still holds the key to Indian tradition. Several famous dances have originated here. All the Indian dances in their traditional forms are taught in Gurukul style. The school a holds festival once a year which is renowned the world over.

Panguni Uttiram

The Hindu festival going by the name Panguni Uttiram falls on the full moon day in the month of 'Phalguna' called Panguni in Tamil (March-April). The moon is then in the asterism 'Uttira' (*Beta Leonis*). Hence the day is considered to be specially favourable for the worship of Śiva.

The festival is also known as *Kalyāṇa Vrata* since goddess Meenakshi is said to have wedded god Sundareśa at Madurai on this day.

It is the belief of the Hindus that the people who observe this Vrata whole-heartedly and sincerely, are blessed with all the boons.

The goddess Meenakshi had her origin[1] in a sacrificial fire in the city of Madurai on a day in the Tamil month of *Adi* (July-August), when the asterism Pooram (*Delta Leonis*) had sway; and ruled over that kingdom. She then commenced a world-round expedition starting from the east. While completing the same in the north-east, Śiva blessed her and promised that he would come to her capital city and marry her.

She thereupon returned to Madurai and was anxiously looking forward to the day when Śiva would come and marry her.

Śiva kept his promise by appearing in her palace on the Adi Puram day which was also a Monday, and married her in the name of Sundareśa. From that time onward this festival has come to be observed every year by the people of southern India, not only in the city of Madurai, but also in almost all the important religious centres in the country.

The Panguni Uttiram day is supposed to be the turning point of the season from winter to summer.

There is also a story current to impress upon the people the importance of this Vrata and it is as follows:

In the Krita or the golden age there lived a pious and highly virtuous king named Raghu, who ruled his country wisely and well. There was neither famine nor sickness during his reign; nor were there any premature or untimely deaths among his subjects.

In ruling over his kingdom, the dictates of Manava Dharma Sastra (Manu Smritis) were closely followed by the king.

Though his subjects were contented and happy for a long time, yet there arose a circumstance which upset the equilibrium and made the people feel ill at ease. A *rakshasi* (female demon) called Dundha visited their houses, troubled their children and was generally harassing them in diverse ways. Unable to prevent her, they at last came to Raghu for help.

The king thereupon sought the advice of the sage Narada,[2] who directed him to observe this Vrata along with his subjects. By doing this, not only was the rakshasi Dundha overpowered, there was also increased wealth and prosperity all over his kingdom.

The temples in which this festival is specially observed are those in Madurai and Tiruvarur in the Tanjore District as well as those at Conjeevaram, Vedaranyam, Tinnevelly, and Perur in the district of Coimbatore.

There is also a myth related to the importance of the observance of this festival at Conjeevaram and it is as follows:

On one occasion Parvati, Śiva's consort, caused Śiva's eyes to be closed by her prowess, and the whole universe was shrouded in darkness as a consequence. Parvati was then deprived of her privileges and position as the consort of Śiva. In order to regain her lost prestige, Parvati is said to have performed a penance at Conjeevaram on this day sitting under a mango tree, invoking the blessings of Śiva who appeared to her and restored her original position to her.

There is also another festival observed by the Hindus as this festive day and it is called the Kāma Dahanam day. The Indian Cupid, Manmatha is said to have been burnt to ashes by the wrath of Śiva on a particular occasion and the myth is as follows:

Once his consort Parvati went to her father's house to attend a sacrifice. Lord Śiva was doing penance at that time. The devas or the celestrial beings, with a view to put an end to the troubles caused by a demon called Tarakasura, desired Manmatha to disturb Śiva's penance so that representations may be made to him about the troubles caused by Tarakasura.

Prompted by the devas, Manmatha aimed at Śiva his arrows, tipped with the petals of his favourite flowers, said to be five in number, with a view to arousing the sleeping passion of Śiva.

Provoked to intense anger by the action of Manmatha, Śiva opened his third or fiery eye and reduced him to ashes. On account of this incident Manmatha has won the immortal name of *Ananga,* that is, 'one without a body.'

Rati,[3] Manmatha's wife (Indian Venus or the goddess of love), aggrieved at losing her lord Manmatha, approached Vishnu and solicited his help. He advised her to go to Sundara Tirtam — a large tank in front of a Śiva temple at Kamarasavalli[4] in the forests of Dandaka, between the river Krishna and the island of Rameswaram, and perform a sacrifice there to propitiate Lord Śiva.

Rati Devi did as advised and underwent severe penance for about forty days.

Śiva, pleased with her austerities, restored to her, her husband, but made him invisible to all save Rati. He is also said to have ordained that the observance of the Kāma dahanam festival in honour of Ananga, should win conjugal felicity for the observer.

Formerly the festival was observed by all classes of people including kings. In course of time, however, it came to be observed only by the Hindus of lower caste.

A bronze representation of Rati[5] appealing to Śiva exists in the temple of Kamarasavalli in the district of Trichinopoly.

A sculptural representation of the form of Manmatha reborn may be seen in the sanctum of Sri Parthasarathy temple at Triplicane in the city of Madras.

The whole scene of the incident is well depicted in the portico near the tank in the Ekambareswara temple at Conjeevaram.

On the east wall of the second prakara in the Adipurisvara temple at Tiruvorriyur[6] near Madras, there is a record of the 9th year of the reign of king Rajakesarivarman *alias* Tribhuvanachakravartin Rajadhirajadeva II (1172-86), mentioning his presence on the occasion of Panguni Uttiram festival in this temple.

NOTES

1   This forms the 4th story of the 64 sports of Sri Sundareswara (vide on *South Indian Shrines* by P.V. Jagadisa Ayyar)

2   For details see *South Indian Shrines* by P.V. Jagadisa Ayyar.

3   Rati is personified as a young and beautiful female, richly attired and decorated, dancing and playing on the *Vina*; and Kāma is represented as a youth with eight arms, attended by four nymphs, — pleasure, affection, passion, and power, — bearing the shell, the lotus, a bow and five arrows, and a banner with the *Makara*,

a figure composed of a goat and a fish, or, as before mentioned, the sign Capricorn, (footnote on page 18 of *Hindu and Mahammadan Festivals*, John Murdoch, 1904).

4 This forms Chapter XVI in *South Indian Shrines* by P.V. Jagadisa Ayyar.

5 For details see *South Indian Shrines* by P.V. Jagadisa Ayyar.

6 This is numbered as 371 of 1911 in the records of the *Madras Epigraphical Department* (Annual Reports published by the Government of Madras) page 432, Vol. 1 of *Inscriptions of the Madras Presidency*, Government of Madras, 1919.

X Chaitra Vishu (The Hindu New Year Day)

The Hindu New Year's Day commences on the first day of the month called Chaitra or Chithirai. It is also called Chaitra Vishu for this reason. The occasion is said to be an auspicious one because, at this time, the sun enters the sign Aries of the Zodiac. The people call the occasion Chaitra Vishu Punyakalam[1], or, the sacred occasion.

The reason why the people in India compute the Indian year from this month when the sun enters Aries — the ram in the signs of the Zodiac — is said to be one philosophically derived from the science of cosmo-genesis. The Sanskrit word for 'ram' is *aja* which means 'that which is not born.' Therefore the sign of the Zodiac under reference stands for the ultimate cause of everything, and consequently the month in which the sun enters this sign is rightly considered to be the first month of the year.

From time immemorial, the Hindu conception of an ideal life has been one of sacrifices and religious observances. Thus the information regarding the appropriate time for the observance of particular rites or ceremonies becomes important. This information is furnished by the Hindu astrologers and astronomers in the form of a calender called *panchangams*.

In ancient times books were very rare and even cudjan[2] leaf manuscripts were not easily available to the vast majority of the people of a village; only the chief priest of the village held a copy of the precious manuscript and it was his duty to apprise the people in his village of the date of observance of a particular festival or Vrata. But in the beginning of the year the people desire to know the position of the various planets with reference to the sun and its effects on men, animals and plants. They also want to know whether the position of the planets would bring them rains in the proper seasons. So the custom of calculating and predicting the planetary influence over the earth through such astrological studies came in vogue.

The days are generally hot and sultry in the month of Chithirai. When a large number of people assemble at a particular place in hot weather, something must be done to counter it. Thus arose the custom of presenting people with cool drinks and fans.

On this festive day people eat margosa[3] flowers, fried or rather charred and mixed with sugar. Apart from the medicinal effect which this preparation has, we may say that this flower belongs to this season and is thus recognised as the harbinger of the coming season.

The custom may also have a deep philosophical significance. The margosa tree rightly symbolises bitterness. Flowers of bitterness blossom forth for the jivas. Let the jivas make it as palatable as possible and take the happenings during the year as light-heartedly as they can.

Coming to the dry facts relating to the new year, we may say that the Tamilians of southern India arrive at their new year day in accordance with the movement of the sun and it is the astronomical year which marks the vernal equinox. The Telugu and the Kannada-speaking people follow the lunar or the luni-solar systems, which precedes the Tamil new year.

The Malayalis of the west coast follow an agricultural year which is known as Kollam Andu, commencing in September when the sun enters the autumnal equinox. It is in this part of the west coast of southern India that very heavy rains fall for nearly nine months in the year.

Though the day commencing each month is considered to be auspicious yet special importance is attached to the occasions, Chaitra Vishu, Tula Ravi, Uttarāyana and Dakshiṇāyana.

The solar year commences from the sun's entrance into aries — the ram. The beginnings of the solar months are determined by the entry of the sun into the other zodiacal signs.

The solar years are recorded in the era of the Kaliyuga. Its years are converted into those of the Christian era by subtracting 3101, from the number of complete years that have lapsed since the beginning of the Kaliyuga. Similarly, the corresponding complete year of the Kaliyuga passed, is arrived at by adding 3101 to the Christian year. Further, by adding 3044 to the year in the Vikrama era and 3179 to the year in the Saka[4] era the corresponding Kaliyuga year is arrived at.

The lunar month Chandrāyanam as opposed to the solar one Sourāyanam is reckoned from the full moon to the full moon. It is invariably determined by the beginning of the bright fortnight of the month, but takes the name of the solar month in which the full moon occurs.

Each month consists of two halves called 'pakshas' and each half is a fortnight in the month. The Śukla paksha or the bright fortnight is the period of the waxing moon while Krishṇa paksha or the dark fortnight is that of the waning moon.

Each of these pakshas again consists of fifteen tithis. A tithi is the time required by the moon to increase its distance from the sun westward by twelve degrees of the zodiac.

As the true motions of the sun and the moon vary with their positions in their orbits the length or duration of a tithi is also variable.

There are names given to these tithis of the fortnight and the fifteenth tithi of the bright fortnight is called the

Purṇamāsi tithi or the full moon, while the fifteenth tithi of the dark fortnight goes by the name Amavāsyā tithi or the new moon. In fact, the full moon and the new moon mark the end bright and dark fortnights of the month respectively.

It is also said that the Chaitra Vishu day or the opening day of the first fortnight of the waxing moon was the occasion chosen by Brahmā to create this world. Hence this day is also known as *yugadhi* or the beginning of a yuga.

This festive day is said to have acquired further importance by the fact that Sri Ramachandra, the hero of the epic Ramayana, had his triumphal entry into Ayodhya after the destruction of the rakshasas, and was crowned there on this day.

There is also an allegorical myth regarding the origin of the Hindu cycle of sixty years and it is in brief as follows:

The sage Narada once betrayed a desire for worldly pleasures and in consequence had to take birth in this mortal world as a woman. He is said to have given birth to sixty children and the Hindu cycle of sixty years is said to have had its origin from those children.

The Hindus believe that the twelve signs of the Zodiac represent twelve planets in the solar system. These planets and centres of consciousness are in the mighty cosmic deity or intelligence called Kālapurusha.[5] In fact, the planets are said to be his head, face, breast, belly, navel, abdomen, genitals, teeth, eyes, knees, ankles and feet.

The Indian calendar is named panchangam since it is comprised of five limbs, and they are (1) the *tithi*, (2) the *varam*, (3) the *nakshatram*, (4) the *yogam* and (5) the *karanam*. A man desiring prosperity pays attention to the tithi. One desirous of long life understands everything about varam or the days of the week. The nakshatrams are resorted to, for expiating sin and the yogam for obtaining immunity from diseases. The karanam is said to secure success for the observer in all his undertakings.

Thus, a proper understanding of planetary influences is essential for controlling them. Hence has arisen the proverb 'wise men rule the stars.'

The[6] story is that once upon a time saint Narada, the celestial celebate, saw a pair of fish in conjugal happiness, while bathing in the sacred Ganges. His passions were excited and he felt a desire to lead a married life. The happiness of a family and the pleasure of children playing about, and a thousand and one things which make life enjoyable, tempted even this citadel of celibacy, this ever-youthful ascetic. He made up his mind to give up his *brahmacharya* and lead the life of a householder. But, he thought, who would give him a wife, and, besides, he had no money to expend on the costly ceremony. What should he do? The best course was to go to Krishna, the king of Dwaraka, and the husband of sixteen thousand one hundred and eight wives! The Lord of Dwaraka could easily spare one, and would not miss her! And he was so fabulously rich that he could easily pay all the expenses! This unholy thought affected the sanctity of the great saint to a certain extent. God, however, felt himself bound to satisfy every desire of his devotees, and Narada stood at the top of them all! All-pervading Vishnu, therefore, organised a counterplot. He took no offence even at so insulting a proposal. Noticing that Narada laid much stress on the large number of his wives and hinted at the impossibility of one man meeting them every day, he asked the saint to go round his houses and to pick up that woman with whom he was not living. Poor Narada! He was not in his senses. He took the bait, and actually went round the whole city, but in every house that Narada visited he found Krishna there, either playing with the children or enjoying the company of his wife in a thousand and one ways. Always happy, always jolly, always in the enjoyment of the highest blessings possible for a married man! That sight still more excited the passions of Narada. He was still thinking how to get a wife when his time for prayer came. As he always bathed and repeated his prayers very punctually, he involuntarily went to the Ganges to bathe. Narada was thinking of going again to Krishna for a wife when he took another dip, and on coming up to the surface of the water was astonished to see that he was turned into a woman! She (now of course *she*) got out of the stream and was going to change her wet clothes, when, lo! a big, tall, stout, manly, good-looking *sanyasi* accosted her. He caught her (Naradi as she must hence be called) by the hand, took her to a cottage and a marriage-by-capture followed. She gave birth to sixty sons one after another, every year! Worried, exhausted, fatigued, bored to death by these numerous sons, at the end of the sixtieth year she involuntarily prayed to lord Vishnu to relieve her of this worldly misery! Repentance did not come too late for the long, eternal (free from death) life of Narada! The sanyasi disappeared and there appeared in his place the glorious Lord of the Universe, god Vishnu, with four hands, holding *sankha, chakra, gada* and *padma,* and said: 'What are your wishes, O eminent woman? They shall be granted!' Naradi looked aghast, looked at the lord again, wiped her eyes and said: 'You know it, my lord. Fool that I was, I thought married life was a bed of roses, full of happiness and pleasures. Save me, my lord!'

'Rise, dear Narada, rise!' was the response. He was transformed into a fully equipped young ascetic in every detail! The god Vishnu embraced him as a friend and asked him to name any other desire, but by this time the sixty sons had gathered round their mother clamouring for food! Narada appealed to Vishnu to silence them. Vishnu gave them the Raj of the world to be enjoyed by turns for one year at a time. This is how each Hindu year has a separate name for a cycle of sixty years. At the end of this cycle falls the Kapila Shasthi, the sacred day on which Naradi was re-transformed into saint Narada!

Here is the list of the sixty sons of Naradi, after whom the lunar years in the cycle are still being called.

Prabhav, Vibhav, Shukla, Paramoda, Prajapati, Angira, Shrimukha, Bhava, Yuva, Dhatu, Ishwar, Bahudanya, Pramathi, Vikrama, Vrisha, Chitrabhanu, Subhanu, Taran, Prartiva, Vyaya, Sarvajit, Sarvadhari, Virodhi, Vikriti, Khara, Nandana, Vijaya, Jaya, Marmath, Durmikha, Hemalambi, Vilambi, Vikari, Sharvar, Plava, Shubakrit, Shobhana, Krodhi, Vishvavasu, Parabhava, Plavanga, Kilaka, Saumya, Sadharana, Virodhikrita, Paridhavi, Pramadi, Ananda, Rakshasa, Nala, Pingala, Kalayukta, Sitdharti, Raudri, Durmati, Dundubhi, Rudhirodgari, Raktakshi, Krodhana, and Akshaya.

NOTES

1   Auspicious time. Any day held sacred on account of the conjunction of certain stars.

2   From Malay *Kajang* means a dressed nipah palm leaf. The cudjan of talipot and palmyra palms are written on with an iron style for accounts, etc. (page 113 of *Manual of the Administration of the Madras Presidency*. Vol.III, Government of Madras, 1893)

3   *Melia Azadirachta* : Melia from a Greek word, on account of its leaves resembling those of the Manna ash and Azadirachta from the Persian name Azad Durukht 'the excellent tree'. This beautiful tree is common everywhere in India, and is as useful as it is ornamental (pp. 33 & 34 of *A Hand Book of the Trees, Shrubs and Herbaceous Plants*, Higginbotham & Co., 1866).

It is said that a certain woman was anxious that her husband should return home soon, when he was preparing to go on a business tour. She sought help from a medical man. He advised her husband to sleep under a tamarind tree on his way out every night during his travels, and to sleep under a *neem* tree on his return journey. He did so and was soon taken ill owing to the unhealthy acid vapours given out by the tamarind. He therefore did not much prolong his journey. He had to turn back. He slept under the neem and by the time he reached home he was quite cured! The oil of the neem is a well-known remedy for leprosy and other skin diseases. During the epidemic of smallpox, festoons of fresh leaves of this tree are hung on the doors of Hindu houses, pp. XXXVI & XXXVII of *Hindu Holidays and Ceremonials*, Gupte, Thacker, Spink & Co., 1919.

4 Saka is the era named after king Salivahana reckoned from A.D. 78. The word Salivahana is from Satavahanas. A line of kings of this dynasty is said to have ruled in the north-west of Mysore under the general name Satakarni and consequently the Mysore state has been spoken of in 1717 as in the Salivahana country. The territory of these Salivahanas extended over the whole of the Dekhan, and Satakarnni is called the lord of Dakshinapatha in the Kshatrapa Rudradaman's inscription. Their chief capital appears to have been at Dhanakataka in the east (Dharanikotta on the river Krishna, now identified with Amaravati in Guntur district); and their chief city in the west was Paithan on the Godavari. *Mysore and Coorg from the Inscriptions,* Rice, Government of Mysore, 1909.

5 There is an illustration of this figure on page 247 of Kalaprakasika, 1917 edition.

6 Pages 98 to 101 of *Hindu Holidays and Ceremonials*, Gupte, Thacker, Spink & Co., 1919.

T he Hindu festival going by the name of Chitra Pournami is observed on the full moon day in the month of Chithirai or chaitra corresponding to the English months of April-May, when the asterism Chitra (*virginis*) holds sway. It is a festival observed to propitiate Chitragupta[1], the chief accountant of Yama, who is believed to record the commissions and omissions by men in order to punish or reward them after their death.

The conception of Chitragupta and his functions is highly allegorical and needs explanation.

The word 'Chitragupta' means a collection of pictures. It goes without saying that the application of this name to the chief accountant of Yama, the god of death, is pregnant with meaning.

The present day gramophone proves that though a man may cease to exist, his voice can be preserved and reproduced any time. By stretching our imagination we can see the possibility of reproducing the thoughts, feelings and actions of each and every one of the individuals during their lifetime if one but knows how to do it. In fact, there is an arrangement in nature by which every incident in the life of individuals, mental, emotional and physical, is recorded in a kind of very fine plastic matter in space and linked to the centre from which it emanated. The aggregations of these incidents are in fact the account of each jiva in the cosmic ledger so to say. At the time of birth and death of an individual, adjustments in his accounts are made, either in the shape of fresh entries or by the removal of certain entries already in existence. The consciousness controlling this adjustment is Yama, the god of death; and his accountant Chitragupta stands figuratively for the cosmic ledger of the accounts of jivas' commissions and omissions — physical, emotional or mental.

In this month, the sun shines in all its splendour, and the moon, which borrows its lustre from the sun, derives the same in full. Hence this day is said to be conducive to the happiness of humanity in general. Further, if the occasion happens to be a Thursday, Saturday or Sunday, it is considered specially auspicious and important.

There is also a myth to emphasise the importance of observing this festival at Madurai[2] and it is as follows:

Brihaspati, the spiritual adviser of the gods, threw up his appointment, since Indra, the celestial king, failed to show proper respect to him. In the absence of the advice of his preceptor, Indra became a great sinner by his commissions and omissions. After some time, Brihaspati relented and returned to duty. He forgave Indra and pointed out to him how he may be purged of all his sins by visiting several holy places. Indra, acting accordingly, came to a forest where he found that all his sins were removed. Looking about himself to find out the cause of his happy deliverance, he found a linga near a tank. Being convinced that the influence radiating from it was the cause of the joy of his heart, he at once sent for Viśvakarma, the celestial architect, and with his aid he erected a splendid shrine for the linga . He also got another shrine erected nearby, containing the figure of Iśwari, Śiva's wife.

Indra then thought of worshipping the god Iśwara and the goddess Iśwari, but had no flowers. He then prayed to the linga and the image of Iśwari, when lo! there suddenly appeared beautiful golden lilies on the surface of the pond. As the day of Indra's worship of Iśwara and Iśwari happened to be the Chitra Pournami day, this festival came to be celebrated at Madurai in a befitting manner. Even now people believe the statement that Indra visits his former place of worship on the Chitra Pournami night every year to worship Iśwara and Iśwari.

The river Chitra which originates in the hills at Kuttalam in the district of Tinnevelly is said to have appeared first on this holy day. So a bath in that river on this occasion is said to confer special merits on people.

In Conjeevaram, there is a special shrine dedicated to Chitragupta, the chief accountant of Yama, the god of death. Both the sculpture in the sanctum and the metallic image of Chitragupta intended for being taken out in procession, bear in one hand a cudjan leaf manuscript and in the other a style, the necessary paraphernalia of an accountant to record the good and bad deeds of men on earth to enable his master Yama to award them heaven or hell after death.

On a pillar in the upper rock-cut cave in the hills of Trichinopoly[3], there is a record of the Chola king Rajakesarivarman (985-1013) gifting land to feed Brahmins and devotees in the nine days' Chitrai festival in the 16th year of his reign.

On the west wall of the Ganeśa shrine in Nedungalanathaswami temple at Tirunedungulam[4], Trichinopoly district, there is another inscription about the same king gifting land for feeding 550 Sivayogins during the Chitrai festival.

NOTES

1 For details see *South Indian Shrines* by P.V. Jagadisa Ayyar.

2 This is the first of the 64 sports of god Sundareśwara of Madurai and it is detailed on *South Indian Shrines* by P.V. Jagadisa Ayyar.

3 This is numbered 412 of 1904 in the records of *Madras Epigraphical Department* (Annual Reports published by the Government of Madras) (pp. 1602 & 1603 of *Inscriptions of the Madras Presidency*, Government of Madras, 1919)

4 This is numbered 687 of 1909 in the records of *Madras Epigraphical Department* (Annual Reports published by the Government of Madras) (p. 1579 of *Inscriptions of the Madras Presidency*, Government of Madras, 1919).

XII   Vaikasi Visaka

The festival Vaikasi Visaka is observed on the day when the asterism Visaka (*Libra*) rules in the month of Vaikasai[1], also called Vaiśakha, corresponding to the English months of May-June. It is a full moon day and Dharmaputra, the god of death, is worshipped. The day is also said to be one on which god Subrahmanya incarnated in this world, making it doubly important and meritorious.

Chaturdasi is the fourteenth tithi counted either from the new moon or full moon. If such a day happens to be a Tuesday in any of the dark fortnights, the occasion is said to be specially favourable for the worship of Dharmaputra and it has the merit of freeing the woroshipper from bodily ailments. Dharmaputra or Dharmarāja, who is worshipped on this occasion, is one of the *Dikpālakas* or guardian angels of the quarters of the earth. He is said to be the guardian of the southern quarter while Indra guards the east. Agni guards the south-east, Niruruthi the south-west, while Varuṇa and Vāyu are the respective guardians of the west and the north-east. Thus we see that the eight directions of the universe are under the control and guardianship of these eight Dikpālakas.

Indra rides on an elephant called Airāvata which is said to be milky white in colour. He is said to exercise control over all the deities except the Trimurti or the Trinity of the Hindus.

Agni is said to ride on a goat. He carries sacrificial offerings made to the other gods in the heavens, causes heat and cold and is said to confer blessings on humanity.

Yama or Dharmarāja, who is the god or angel of death, is said to ride on a buffalo. He judges of the actions of the jivas on this earth and rewards or punishes them after their death, assigning them either heaven or hell according to their deserts. He is assisted in this task by his accountant Chitragupta.

Niruruthi, who is said to ride on a demon, is the chief of the rakshasas. His function is to award suitable benefits to people in return for the performance of sacrifices by them to propitiate the gods.

Varuṇa is the lord of the rains and he is said to ride on a sea monster.

Vāyu, who is said to ride on an antelope, presides over the air and diffuses good and bad scents everywhere.

Kubera rides on a horse and confers wealth of various kinds on those worshipping him.

Esana rides on a bull and exercises general destructive powers.

This is a month in which the days are extremely hot and sultry. Ponds dry up and plants wither away rapidly. Hence the ancient sages have laid down that acts of charity such as presentation of cooked rice mixed with curd, followed by cool and delicious drinks during the days of this month, would confer longevity on the children, remove sterility in women, cure various afflictions and, in short, would secure for the donor religious merit of a very high order. Presentation of umbrellas, fans and leather sandals as well as the watering of plants and trees in general and Tulasi plant (*ocymum sanctum*) and the Aswatha tree (*ficus religiosa*) in particular, are considered to be acts of great religious merit. Wise, indeed, have been the ancient sages, who have laid down rules conducive to the general well-being of the people.

Certain places are considered to be specially important for such acts of charity. Swamimalai[2], near Kumbakonam in the Tanjore district, is one among those. There is a myth reflecting its importance which is as follows:

An asura named Arikesa was giving Indra a lot of trouble. Do what he could, he was not able to get rid of the demon and his troubles. At a loss to know what to do and in great despair, he paid visits to the various religious centres of the land. When he came to Swamimalai and worshipped the presiding deity of the temple there, he is said to have been blessed with the strength to shake off the demon and win back the kingdom that the latter had usurped!

The observance of this festival at Tirumazhuvadi near Tanjore is considered specially important for the reason that Śiva had once performed a *mazhu* or lance dance at this place on the Vaikasi Visaka day. Further, it is said to be the place where Śiva's sacred bull had its incarnation on this festive occasion.

Alwartirunagari in the district of Tinnevelly is the next important place for observing this festival. Once there lived a famous Vaishnava saint called Nammalwar.[3] He is said to have rendered the sacred Vedas of the Hindus into Tamil. As he was born on the Vaikasi Visaka day at Alwartirunagari, the observance of this festival there is considered specially meritorious.

There is an image representing the Narasimha avatāra (incarnation) of Vishnu, in the hill temple of Simhachalam[4] in Vizianagaram. On all days of the year, it remains coated with sandal paste, but on the Vaikasi Visaka day, the paste is scrubbed off and the form is available for view. It can be viewed again only on the next Vaikasi Visaka day. People flock to have a view of the figure on this day.

On the outer wall of the northern enclosure of the Tanjore temple there is a record[5] of the Chola king Rajendradeva (1050-63) making provision for a daily allowance of paddy to a troop of actors who enacted the drama *Rajarajeswara nataka* on the occasion of the Vaikasi festival in the 6th year of his reign. On the rock outside the north prakara of the Ratnachaleswara temple at Ratnagiri,[6] Trichinopoly district, there is an inscription relating to the 16th year, 340th day of Tribhuvanachakravartin Konerumelkondan, making a gift of land for Vaikasi Tirunal.

NOTES

1. Now the spirit of the time is precisely that which marked a great part of the month of February among the Romans, and the name of the month itself is said to have been derived from its dedication by Numa to Februus, the god of lustrations, for in that month it was necessary to purify the city and pay to the Dii Manes the oblations that were their due. According to some, the name is derived from the verb 'februor,' which means to be cleansed or purified. The connection between lustrations and obsequial rites is another analogy, and in consonance with this opinion, the Feralia, or worship of the manes, was celebrated for several days in February ending with the 17th, or according to some, with the 23rd. The month was thence also called the *Feralis Mensis*. This similarity of time and of purposes can scarcely have been accidental, and there can be no reasonable doubt that the Feralia of the Romans and the *sraddha* of the Hindus, the worship of the manes and of the Pitris, have a common character and a common origin. Pages 27 and 28 of *Hindu and Mahammadan Festivals*, John Murdoch, 1904.

2. This is dealt with in *South Indian Shrines*, P.V. Jagadisa Ayyar.

3. For a short summary of this Alwar's life on *South Indian Shrines*, P.V. Jagadisa Ayyar.

4. This forms Chapter XLII of *South Indian Shrines* by P.V. Jagadisa Ayyar.

5. This is numbered as 55 of 1893 in the records of the *Madras Epigraphical Department* (Annual Reports published by the

Government of Madras) (p. 1408 Vol. II of *Inscriptions of the Madras Presidency*, Government of Madras, 1919)

6 This is numbered as 171 of 1914 in the records of the *Madras Epigraphical Department* (Annual Reports published by the Government of Madras) (p. 1520 Vol. III of *Inscriptions of the Madras Presidency*, Government of Madras, 1919)

XIII   Adi Puram

This Hindu festival of Adi Puram is celebrated in all Hindu temples in southern India in the month called Adi or Ashadha, corresponding to the English months of July-August, when the asterism Puram (*Delta Leonis*) is in the ascendency. The festival is observed to propitiate the goddess Śakti Devi who is said to have come into this world on this occasion to bless the people. People therefore worship her in order to secure happiness not only for themselves but also for their loved ones.

If the festival falls on a Friday, the occasion is considered to be highly auspicious, and the people worship the goddess in a more special way.

It is said that there are eight *Nidhis* or *Śaktis* (Forces of nature) in the universe and they are controlled by Devi, the goddess of the Hindus. The eight magical arts, called in Hindu mystic parlance the *Ashta Mahā Siddhis,* are derived from a knowledge of those forces. They are (1) *Animā* or the art of entering into a foreign body, (2) *Mahimā* or the art of increasing the bulk of one's body, (3) *Garuna* or the art of rendering small things tremendously ponderous, (4) *Laghimā* or the art of lifting with ease the largest and the heaviest substances, (5) *Prapti* or the art of gaining access through a small hole to Brahma's heaven, (6) *Prakamya* or the art of transubstantiating and entering into various worlds of tenuous matter, procuring all things needful from these and ascertaining the localities of various substances, (7) *Isatwam* the art of creating, protecting and destroying the world as well as rendering the planets obedient to the will, and (8) *Vasitwam* the art of bringing all created beings under subjection including Indra and the various gods.

The eight Nidhis[1] are also called by eight different names with characteristics peculiar to each. The Nidhi called *Padma* is said to be presided over by Lakshmi and people attaining this Nidhi secure prowess and skill in warfare and also command the wealth of all mortals.

The Nidhi going by the name *Mahapadma* secures the command over all precious gems in the universe. It is meant for one having yogic tendencies in him.

The Nidhi named *Makara* shapes the character of the individual and secures for him success in military operations and royal favour.

The Nidhi called *Kachapa* brings success in all business undertakings and makes the individual the beloved of one and all.

While the Nidhi *Mukunda* develops fine aesthetic instincts in the individual, and the one called *Nanda* secures for him good harvest and immunity from wants.

The Nidhi called *Nila* is said to lead to all sorts of enjoyments and the one named *Sanka* ensures self-realisation and eternal bliss.

The two Nidhis Sanka and Padma confer mundane enjoyments and heavenly bliss on individuals. The wealth secured by Padma Nidhi makes worldly enjoyments possible and the yogic powers conferred by Sanka Nidhi result in bliss arising from self-realisation.

As these two Nidhis control the other Nidhis, sculptural representations of only these two Nidhis are placed at the sides of temple entrances in southern India.

In a portico called 'Ashta Siddhi Mandapam' in Madurai, we have sculptural representations of these eight Siddhis or

Śaktis. The reason is that Sri Sundareśwara, the presiding deity of the Madurai Temple, is said to have manifested these powers to the people of this world on one occasion. The details of the incident are given in a book called 'Halasya Mahatmiyam', also called 'Tiruvelayadal Puranam' in Tamil. Sixty-four[2] miracles performed by Sri Sundareśwara are recorded in this work.

According to a myth, the goddess of the universe took a human form on the Adi Puram day in a miraculous manner. A Vaishṇava saint called Periyalwar[3] of Srivilliputtur had no issues. He prayed to the goddess Lakshmi for children and his wish was fulfilled by her in the following manner. Alwar was ploughing his fields one day when he came upon a lovely female child while turning the first furrow. Delighted at the precious find, he hastened to his home with it. He gave it to his wife, and named it Andal. The presiding deity of Srirangam temple, Sri Ranganath, is said to have accepted Andal as his wife when she grew up.

The festival is observed with great éclat in the temples of Madurai, Srivilliputtur, Tinnevelly, Vedaranyam, Negapatam, Jambukeswaram, Tiruvadi, Kumbakonam, Tiruvadaimarudhur, Mayavaram, Srivanjiyam and Tiruvannamalai. In the famous religious centre Chidambaram also, this Puram festival is observed not in the month Adi (July-August), but in the month Arpisi (November). The observance is said to be rather unique. There is also an inscription[4] in the west gopuram of the temple and it is dated Saka 1517. The village called Poorappettai is mentioned in connection with the observance of this festival as stated above.

It is noteworthy that all festivals are held only once in a year and no festival is held twice. All the important festivals are observed throughout the country at the same time. As the religious festivals of the Hindus are closely connected with the movements of the stars and planets, correct information regarding the time at which the observation should take place is highly essential if at all the observances are to be efficacious. Hence great stress is laid on the accuracy of the information to be recorded in the Hindu almanacs or Panchāngams by the astronomers.

As several systems of computation have arisen with the lapse of time, some following the heliocentric system, and some following the geocentric system and so on, differences of opinion have also arisen regarding the time of the observance of Hindu rites and ceremonies. But the principle on which these observances are based is the same and we find no differences in opinion in this regard. Further, in the observance of most of the important religious festivals, we find no differences of opinion among the astronomers.

The Vedas and the Agamas say that the performance of a definite number of religious festivals is essential for the welfare of a country. The number of such festivals varies with the different sects of Hindus. It is recorded[5] in the second prakāra of Sri Tyagaraja temple at Tiruvarur in Tanjore that fifty-six festivals are to be observed every year.

NOTES

1 These are described on pp. 288 to 291 (Chapter LXVIII) of *Markandeya Purāṇa*, M.N. Dutt, 1897.

2 A summary of these appears in *South Indian Shrines* by P.V. Jagadisa Ayyar.

3 For a life of this saint consult in *South Indian Shrines* by P.V. Jagadisa Ayyar, Madras Times Publishing Company Ltd., 1920.

4 This is numbered as 360 of 1913 in the records of the *Madras Epigraphical Department* (Annual Reports published by the

Government of Madras) (page 147, Vol. I of *Inscriptions of the Madras Presidency*, Government of Madras, 1919).

5 This is numbered as 269 of 1901 (No. 911, page 1349, Vol. I of *Inscriptions of the Madras Presidency*, Government of Madras, 1919).

Vyāsa Puja is a ceremony observed on the full moon day in the month of Ashadha called Adi in Tamil, corresponding to the English months of July-August, mainly for the general welfare of the world. It is a ceremony more important to the sanyasis (ascetics) and others, who have renounced the world, than to the worldly-minded men. Renunciation implies there are no restricted sympathies, affections and responsibilities which worldly men have in the shape of family ties and responsibilities, etc. They have in fact unrestricted responsibilities, to wit, the welfare of humanity as a whole. Hence the sanyasis and others, who have renounced the world and its pleasures, perform Vyāsa Puja to bring to humanity the blessings of the mighty sage Vyāsa, the author of the famous Indian epic *Mahabharata*.

The reason why the sage Vyāsa of all the sages is worshipped by the sanyasis and others who have renounced the world, is that the Adi Śankaracharya of the Hindus is believed to be Vyāsa himself incarnated as that mighty teacher and consequently none deserves the puja better than him. In fact, knowledgeable the people say that the worship of Vyāsa is the worship of Adi Śankara and the worship of Adi Śankara is the worship of Vyāsa. Anyhow the sanyasis, as the followers in the footsteps of Adi Śankara, whom they have taken as their guru, must worship him and they worship him by worshipping Vyāsa on the Vyāsa Puja day.

The mode of observance of this puja is interesting and noteworthy. Rice is spread on a piece of new cloth and over it are placed lime fruits to draw the presence of Adi Śankara and his four disciples on. After the puja ceremony is over, the rice is distributed to people which is to be taken home and mixed with the stock kept there. Let us pause to consider what significance might have been attached to this modus operandi.

Lakshmi, the goddess of wealth, is said to reside in rice and new clothes. On auspicious occasions, her presence is invoked on a bed of paddy or rice which forms the staple article of food in the land. Further, it has been the timeworn custom of the Hindus that lime fruits (one or two of them) should be taken as presents when paying visits to kings and men in power to solicit favours. So we may say that lime fruits are intended to symbolise success in any undertaking.

For the performance of any of the ceremonies, we need wealth which is bestowed by Lakshmi. We pray for success in our undertakings, symbolising the same by using lemons. So the modus operandi in Vyāsa Puja is perhaps for invoking the presence of and soliciting the blessings of Lakshmi accompanied by her husband Vishṇu, for success in the undertaking.

Two centres were established in southern India, one at Kumbakonam[1] in the Tanjore district and the other at Sringeri[2] in the Mysore state, to perpetuate the memory of Sri Sankaracharya and this festival is observed with great éclat every year at these places. People assemble there in large numbers to witness the performance of the puja and to obtain the blessings of the sage Vyāsa.

There is a hall in front of the central shrine[3] of Vidyaśankara in Sringeri. It is supported by twelve pillars. The architectural design is such that the rays of the sun fall on each of the pillars in the order of the solar months. Here is a practical problem for the would-be Hindu yogis to solve and for the advanced yogis to admire.

As the whole ceremony of Vyāsa Puja hinges on the great personage Adi Śankaracharya, a short sketch of his life and work would not be out of place here. He is believed to have been a sage and a religious reformer. Some even go to the extent of saying that he was an incarnation of Śiva (one of the Hindu Trinity). He was born at a village called Kaladi on the river Alwaye, also called Churni, in Malabar. It was a day in the month of Vaiśakha, when the constellation Punarvasu is, said to be highly favourable for the birth of a great soul in this world. This marvellous child grew up to become one of the greatest religious teachers in the world.

The fifth day of the new moon fortnight on which Sri Śankara was born to Sivaguru, a pious Brahmin and his wife Aryamba, is a red letter day in the annals of south Indian religious history, going by the name Śankarajayanti day. His philosophical treatises are none the worse for the onslaught made on them by rival religious thinkers. In fact, his commentaries on many of the philosophical treatises have resisted the attacks made on the treatises themselves and have kept them unimpaired and free from corruption, through the ages.

Sri Śankara is said to have received his spiritual initiation from Sri Govinda Bhagavatpada. He is also said to have made a tour throughout India for the purpose of reviving the religion of the Hindus since he thought that it had become corrupt by the pernicious teachings of certain new religious cults.

Three schools of thought are prominent in the Vedānta philosophy, viz., Advaita, Dvaita and Vishiṣṭādvaita. Of these, the Advaita school of philosophy owes its origin to Sri Śankaracharya and the other two to Madhvācharya and Rāmānujacharya respectively.

Sri Śankara's philosophy, put in a nutshell, is simply this. There is only one reality, viz., Brahman, the Unqualified

Absolute. When the limitations imposed on jivas by layers and layers of matter are cast off, the feeling of separation of jiva and Brahman ceases to exist and the liberated jiva (if we can use the word since it shows separating)becomes one with Brahman.

The Dvaitavādins of the Madhva school of philosophy hold that there cannot be oneness of consciousness and that jivas will always be feeling a separate existence from that supreme intelligence going by the name God, though there may be several degrees of intensity in that feeling.

The followers of Vishiṣṭādvaitavād assert that the Absolute is an identity qualified by diversity. jiva or soul shares omniscience and bliss with God yet it is different from God in being an atomic mode (prakāra) of God.

Sri Śankara is said to have had many disciples and of those, Padmapada, Hastamalaka, Totaka and Mandana Miśra are considered to have been the most prominent. He is said to have visited Prayag and Varanasi, and finally to have brought from Kailasa, the abode of Śiva, five *sphatika* (crystal) lingas or phallic symbols. They go by the names of *Bhoga linga* or the linga that could confer on the worshippers enjoyments of every kind, *Mukti linga* or the linga that could ensure for its devotee liberation from the wheel of birth and death, *Vara linga* or the linga that could confer boons of all kinds, *Yoga linga* or the linga that could bestow on souls the bliss resulting from the unification of consciousness of the jivas and the Iśvara, and the *Moksha linga* or the linga that could give extreme bliss or *ānanda*, said to be the birth right of ātma, the soul of human beings. These lingas now remain located respectively at Sringeri, Kethara-Kshetra, Nepal, Kumbakonam and Chidambaram. Sri Śankara's seat at Sringeri is known as Śāradā Peetha. The reason for the name is that the goddess of learning, Saraswati is said to abide in that sanctum sanctorum, radiating her influence for the welfare of humanity, having been installed there by Sri Śankara for the purpose.

Sri Śankara is said to have created many influence-radiating centres in southern India choosing many temples for the purpose. Consequently people visiting those temples are said to return home greatly benefited by the magnetic influence pervading the temple atmosphere.

Sri Śankara has written commentaries or *Bhashyas* on the Bhāgavat Gita, the Vyāsa Sutras and on Upanishads. These help students to unravel the mysteries contained in those works of abstruse metaphysical problems. Sri Śankara appears to have had two classes of disciples going by the names *Srotas* and *Smartas*. The former were passive listeners because they were new pupils just admitted and the latter were the advanced and acknowledged disciples, to whom regular instruction and training in Brahma Vidyā was given. The Smartas of the present time are the descendants and followers of the Smarta class disciples. It appears that the Srotas became Smartas in course of time by the progress made by them in knowledge.

The word *Śruti* comes from *śru,* to hear, and the word *Smriti* comes from *smru,* to remember. Hence have arisen the words the Srutis and the Smritis of the Hindus.

Sri Śankara is said to have visited Badrinath, Kedarnath, Nepal, Ayodhya, Dwaraka and Gokula in northern India. In southern India, he visited Jambukesvaram,[4] Tirupati[5] and Conjeevaram.[6] In the last place, Sri Śankara is said to have designed the plan of the town, in the form of Śri Chakra, with the temple in the middle.

NOTES

1 Originally it was in Conjeevaram that this seat was located. It was subsequently removed to Kumbakonam during the days of the Maratha kings of Tanjore from this place. The circumstances that led to the transfer of this are mentioned in *South Indian Shrines* by P.V. Jagadisa Ayyar.

2 This place is described in detail in Chapter XLIII of *South Indian Shrines* by P.V. Jagadisa Ayyar.

3 For details see *South Indian Shrines* by P.V. Jagadisa Ayyar.

4 This is described in Chapter XXV of *South Indian Shrines* by P.V. Jagadisa Ayyar.

5 This is described in Chapter XXXIV of *South Indian Shrines* by P.V. Jagadisa Ayyar.

6 This is described in Chapter II of *South Indian Shrines* by P.V. Jagadisa Ayyar.

Avani Mulam

The religious day of Avani Mula falls in the month of Bhādrapada called Avani in Tamil corresponding to the English months of August- September. This month and especially this day is said to be under the influence of the asterism Mulam (*Scorpionis*) and its presiding deity is an asura named Nirrithi.

The Hindus believe that there are two forces or influences working in the universe, one favouring the evolution of souls and the other hindering it. There are intelligences working in both these currents of influences. As the universe is governed by strict justice, certain periods are under the control of one force and certain periods under the other. The night hours, between midnight and 4 a.m., are said to be favourable for the play of forces adverse to human spiritual progress. Similarly this month, falling under the influence of the asura Nirrithi, has a preponderance of asuric[1] tendencies not favourable for the progress of human souls. Hence, to ward off the harm and evil effects resulting from the asuric tendencies of the asura Nirrithi, human beings are advised to lead a religious life which would enable them to find out and cast off subtle asuric influences sown into them.

There is also a myth attached to the origin of the importance of this event and one of its versions is as follows:

Once, there ruled in Madurai a king named Arimadhava Pandyan. During his reign[2] there was a great drought and the river Vaigai was completely dry for a long time.

It was believed that Indra, the god of the celestials, displeased with the ruler of Madurai, had caused the drought in his kingdom. One day, all of a sudden, a short but heavy shower caused slight flood in the river. The king Arimadhava Pandyan wanted to stop the flow of water towards and into the ocean, so that not a drop of the precious water might be lost. This was possible only by getting a dam constructed across the river. In order to ensure this, he divided the task among the people of Madurai by assigning to each of them the construction of a particular portion of dam.

A small portion of the dam was allotted to an old woman whose vocation was to prepare and sell pudding. She was a good and pious woman deeply devoted to Sundareśa, the guardian deity of Madurai.

Called upon by the royal ministers to finish the work allotted to her with threats of severe punishment if she made any delay, the old woman was terrified and prayed to Sundareśa, her only refuge, when she could not secure the services of any workman on account of the heavy demand for labourers just then from every quarter of the town.

In the guise of a workman, with a basket on the head and a spade in his hand, Lord Sundareśa hastened to relieve his devotee of her anxiety. Finding a workman almost at her door, ostensibly with no work on hand for the day, the old woman approached him with the request to finish the work allotted to her by the evening. The woman had no money to give to the workman and all that he desired was something to satisfy his hunger. An agreement was made that the workman was bound to finish the portion of the embankment assigned to the woman and she was to give him pudding whenever he felt hungry after hard work.

The workman ate enough pudding to satisfy his hunger, and carried with him enough to satisfy his hunger if he felt so subsequently. When he came to the spot where the other labourers were hard at work, instead of attending to the work allotted to the woman, he distributed the pudding among the workmen, chatted with them merrily and was in fact retarding instead of hastening the construction work.

The officials in charge remonstrated with him, threatened him with punishment but to no avail. He would not work, but would boast that he could work wonders. He would often go to the woman with the tale of weariness and hunger and come back to the spot loaded with pudding to be distributed afresh among the workmen there.

When the sun had set, the work of constructing the embankment was almost over except for the small portion allotted to the old woman. Water was escaping through this gap, making it broader and broader each minute, washing away the adjacent portion completed by the other workmen.

At this juncture, the king came on horseback to inspect the construction site. He halted when he came to the gap through which the precious water was flowing out. Blazing with anger, the king enquired about the defaulter. The officials pointed out to the lazy workman, who was just measuring his steps and was counting them, with a basket on his head which contained a handful of earth. The king beckoned him to appear before him and when he came near he hit him on his back with a cane. Every living creature there and elsewhere in the world felt the blow given to the workman and writhed in pain! The king, by punishing Lord Sundareśa, punished not only himself but also every living creature, since he abides in every living thing on earth.

When the workman received the smart blow on his back, he dropped the small quantity of earth he held in the basket, at the gap, when lo! there was no gap to be seen in the embankment!

Stupefied with astonishment at the miracle wrought by the seeming workman, the king was petrified for a moment. When he regained his senses, he searched for the workman throughout the city in vain for He had vanished from human sight!

By a flash of intuition, corroborated by a voice from the sky, the king knew that the seeming workman was verily his patron Lord Sundareśa who came to teach him a lesson for having unwittingly punished his minister Manikkavachakar, who had spent certain state funds in the services of the Lord of the Avadayarkoil temple.

The episode of the old woman and her pudding shows the physical link formed between her and the Lord with which she was to be drawn nearer and nearer to Him till she was merged in his all-pervading consciousness.

As the incident narrated above is said to have taken place on the Avani Mulam day, special importance[3] is attached to it.

Though the day is observed as a festive occasion throughout the land, special importance is attached to Madurai, the scene of the incidents and consequently, the festival is observed there in all its grandeur. With a golden basket and a golden spade[4], the god Sundareśa is taken in procession on this festive day from the river *ghat* to the temple amidst much rejoicing of the people.

NOTES

1 From Sanskrit *as* = to be : life. Demons and giants, who, like the Titans of the Greeks, made war against the gods.

2 This forms the 61st story of *Halasya Mahatmya* (Sanskrit) or Tiruvilayadal Purāṇa (Tamil) which records the 64 sports of god Sundareśa at Madurai. See also *South Indian Shrines* by P.V. Jagadisa Ayyar.

3 This also accounts for the festival being performed in most of the Tamil districts in southern India.

4 This forms part of the jewels belonging to god Sundareśa at Madurai. For details see *South Indian Shrines* by P.V. Jagadisa Ayyar.

XVI   Vara Lakshmi Vrata

The Hindu festival going by the name 'Vara Lakshmi Vrata' is celebrated on the last Friday of the bright fortnight in the month of Ashadha, also called Adi, which corresponds to the English months of July-August. It is a festival to propitiate the goddess Lakshmi, the consort of Vishṇu, one of the Hindu Trinity. The name Vishṇu really means 'pervading everywhere,' and Lakshmi, his consort, is symbolical of the forces found everywhere. Eight forces or energies are recognised and they are known as *Sri* (Wealth), *Bhu* (Earth), *Sarasvati* (learning), *Priti* (love), *Kirti* (Fame), *Śanti* (Peace), *Tushṭi* (Pleasure) and *Pushṭi* (Strength). Each one of these forces is called a Lakshmi and all the eight forces are called the *Ashṭa Lakshmis[1]* or the eight Lakshmis of the Hindus. Vishṇu is also called Ashṭa Lakshmi Padhi which is equivalent to saying that he is the asylum for the eight-Lakshmis or forces. In fact, Vishṇu representing the preservative aspect of the universe, radiates these forces from him. These forces are personified and worshipped as Lakshmis, since abstract force is beyond the comprehension of the ordinary people. As health, wealth and prosperity depend upon the rythmic play of these forces, the worship of Lakshmi is said to be to obtain these three. Only a woman can sympathise with women. Lakshmi is a woman. So she will more readily sympathise with women. Hence this festival is observed largely by women, invoking the blessings of Lakshmi on them, their husbands and their children.

There are myths relating to the importance of observing this festival on the Friday which immediately precedes or falls on the full moon day of the month Ashadha, and it is as sketched below:

On one occasion, Parvati and Parameśwara were engaged in a game of chess[2]. Parvati was winning game after game, but Parameśwara is said to have claimed the victory at each and every one of the games, wantonly, to her intense chagrin. So Parvati wanted to have an umpire and one Chitranemi, a creation of Parameśwara, was chosen. As an underling of Parameśwara, he sided with him most unjustly. This provoked Parvati's anger and she cursed Chitranemi that he should become a leper for discharging his duty in most unfair manner.

When Chitranemi begged Parvati's forgiveness and Parameśwara added his entreaties to it, she is said to have relented and modified the curse by adding that he would be cured of his leprosy by observing the Vara Lakshmi Vrata. By doing this Chitranemi was, it is said, rid of the loathsome disease.

The history of the origin of the Vara Lakshmi Vrata is rather interesting. Lakshmi is said to have visited a pious woman by name Sarmadi, living in the city of Kuntinapura in Magadha (Bihar), in one of her dreams and expressed her satisfaction at her devotion to her children. When she woke up from her sleep, she took a bath and worshipped Lakshmi to ensure her blessings. When the other ladies heard of her dream and her worship of Lakshmi, they too began to worship her, and the custom is then said to have spread everywhere throughout the land in course of time.

The leaves of certain plants and trees are supposed to be the favourite materials for use in worshipping certain deities. The leaves of the bael tree are considered to be specially acceptable to Śiva while Vishṇu is said to have a preference for sweet basil—Tulasi plant. Similarly a kind of grass called durva[3] grass in Sanskrit, aruhu in Tamil, hariali grass in

Canarese (*Cynodon Dactylon*), is said to be specially acceptable to Lakshmi. So people gather this grass to worship her on this Vrata day. The ancient alchemists believed that a white variety of this grass was available which could be used to convert baser metals into gold! This fact, perhaps, was instrumental in creating the belief that the grass was acceptable to Lakshmi. At any rate there is no gainsaying the fact that a decoction of the root of this grass was considered a potent drink to allay the heat generated in the body by yoga practices.

As prosperity and adversity are antagonistic to each other, so Lakshmi has her contrast in goddess Ava Lakshmi[4] who represents adversity. Ava Lakshmi is always spoken of as the elder sister of Lakshmi. It means that adversity is the elder sister of prosperity. Even in the Puraṇas it is said that when the ocean of milk was churned by the devas and the asuras, Ava Lakshmi or adversity was the first outcome and Lakshmi the next. Herein is illustrated a sublime philosophical dictum. In the absence of pain, pleasure will have no existence. Unless a man has felt the sun's intense heat, he cannot experience the pleasure of resting in the cool shade. In the absence of hunger, relish for food ceases to exist. Similarly a man feels the pleasures of prosperity because he has experienced adversity before, remembers it now and contrasts it with his present position. Hence, adversity is said to be the elder sister of prosperity.

It is said that people were once worshipping this elder sister adversity. Fearing that she might show her nature to them if propitiated with worship, they are said to have given it up.

This goddess Ava Lakshmi has another name 'Kapila Patni' which means 'the wife of Kapila', a sage who married her since no one else would wed her. She is said to reside in pipal trees and so people dare not touch them on days other than Saturdays, when Lakshmi is supposed to be present in those trees, visiting her elder sister and, consequently, no harm could come to them as long as she is there to protect them.

Special temples dedicated to Mahā Lakshmi exist in Doddagaddavalli in Mysore as well as in Kolhapur in Maharashtra.

Lakshmi is said to have worshipped Lord Śiva in the temples of Tiruvadi[5] near Tanjore, in Tiruninriyur near Vaithiswarankoil, in Tiruthengur near Tiruvarur[6] and Tiruppathur in the Ramnad district, and consequently these places are considered to be specially important for the observance of Vara Lakshmi Vrata and other Vratas invoking the blessings of Lakshmi.

NOTES

1   These are fully described on pages 187 & 189 of *South Indian Gods and Goddesses*, Rao Bahadur H. Krishna Sastrigal, Government of Madras, 1916

2   Sanskrit *chaturanga* (*chatur* = four and *anga* = member).

3   This is one of the commonest grasses, growing everywhere in great abundance. It forms the greater part of the food of cattle in this country. It is the prettiest and most lasting grass for planting lawns, etc. Its usefulness added to its beauty induced the Hindus to celebrate it in their writings. Page 238, *A Hand Book of the Trees, Shrubs and Herbaceous Plants*, Higginbotham & Co., 1866.

It is a sand-binding and bund-protecting grass. It stands heavy rolling. By constantly rolling or allowing people to walk over hariali lawns the growth of the grass is doubly encouraged, directly by helping the prostrate habit of hariali and indirectly by hardening the soil and killing all weeds. It grows well and luxuriously in all kinds of soils from a poor light sea-sand to a rich heavy clay soil, provided it gets a good supply of water at the commencement of its growth together with bright sunlight and thorough drainage. No other grass in India has such a wonderful development of root like subterranean stem growth.

4   A figure of this goddess is illustrated in plate 135 together with a description on pages 216 and 217 of *South Indian Gods and Goddesses*, Rao Bahadur H. Krishna Sastrigal, Government of Madras, 1916. Also see page 363 of Vol. I, part II of *Elements of Hindu Iconography*, T.A. Gopinatha Rao, Law Printing House, Madras, 1914 & 1916.

5   This forms Chapter XVIII of *South Indian Shrines* by P.V. Jagadisa Ayyar.

6   This forms Chapter XIX of *South Indian Shrines* by P.V. Jagadisa Ayyar.

XVII   Upakarmam

A bird is called *Dwija* or twice born, since it is first born as an egg and then comes out of it as a bird. Similarly, a Brahmin is called a Dwija since he has the ordinary birth as well as the spiritual birth by the ceremony called *upanayanam* performed for him by his parents and family *guru* or preceptor.

The upanayanam has a deep spiritual significance. With the ordinary eyes, men are able to see everything belonging to the physical world. But the Hindus believe in the existence of fourteen *lokas*[1] (worlds) also called *talas.* Each loka is like this physical world of ours full of conscious entities as well as minerals, vegetables and animals.

The fourteen lokas are named Bhur-loka, Bhuvar-loka, Suvar-loka, Mahar-loka, Janar-loka, Tapar-loka, Satya-loka, Brahma-loka, Pitri-loka, Soma-loka, Indra-loka, Gandharva-loka, Rakshasa-loka and Yaksha-loka.

Represented by the expression tala, they go by the names Atala, Vitala, Sutala, Karatala, Rasatala, Mahatala and Patala, and seven other names.

The end and aim of a human being should be to vivify his consciousness in each and every one of these worlds and work there, just as he works here in this physical world. This is in fact said to be the *summum bonum* of life in this world.

The word 'upanayanam' means additional eye. By his knowledge of things beyond mundane, the guru (preceptor) becomes an eye-opener to the youth who begins to see the next higher world. In fact this ceremony was performed for Arjuna by Sri Krishṇa in the battlefield. By strenuous application day after day, the youth develops this new sight more and more till it is fully open. In this way he is said to open and develop seven sights before completing his evolution.

The thread[2] worn by Brahmins symbolises the play of spiritual forces in his finer bodies radiating the spiritual light around him. The carbon filament within an electric bulb may rightly be compared to this sacred thread worn by the Hindus which in fact represents seven such threads of fire in his seven bodies in as many worlds of fine matter.

It is laid down in Hindu Dharma Śastras that a portion of everything earned or acquired should be distributed as charity. The Brahmins acquire and store only spiritual force which is represented by the sacred thread called *poonuℓ*. So by distributing these sacred strings they are supposed to distribute a portion of the spiritual force acquired by them. People increase their stock of spiritual energy by wearing these threads.

The Upakarma religious ceremony is performed by the Hindus following the Yajurveda, in the month of Śravana, called Avani in Tamil, corresponding to the English months of August-September, on the full moon day if it happens to be free from defects. If the full moon day in Avani is not free from defects, then the full moon day in the month of Purattasi (September-October) is selected. If that day too is wanting in purity required for the purpose, then the full moon day in the month of Adi (July-August) is selected.

The people who follow the Rig Veda observe the ceremony in the month of Avani when the asterism Śravana (*aquiloe*) is in the ascendency.

The people who follow the Sāma Veda observe the ceremony in the same month Avani but on the day when the asterism Hasta (*corvi*) and the tithi Panchami prevail.

The recitation of the Vedas on this day is said to be very meritorious. Libations of water are poured to propitiate the manes of the departed souls and the sages who had taken the trouble to preserve and hand over to posterity the Vedas — the source of religious beliefs and ceremonies.

The Vedas are said to have worshipped Lord Śiva called Iśwara in several places. The most important of those places are the temples at Vedaranyam[4] in the district of Tanjore, Tiruvazhundur near Kuttalam in the same district, Tirukkalukunram[5] in the Chingleput district, Tiruvedikkudi near Tanjore and Tiruppanaivasa near Shiyali.

It is said that once the Vedas were revealed to the sages by God himself at Tiruvottiiyur near Conjeevaram. The goddess is said to have had the mysteries of the Vedas revealed to her by Iśwara at a place called Uttarakosamangai near Ramnad. Further, God is said to have chanted the Vedas at a place called Tiruthuruthi near Mayavaram, in the guise of a Brahmachāri youth.

NOTES

1   Sanskrit *lus* = to see world. Generally means seven upper worlds allotted for the residence of different species of animated beings. Pages 435 and 436 *Manual of the Administration of the Madras Presidency*. Vol.III, Government of Madras, 1893.

2   The sacred thread is called Yajnopavitam (*yajna* = sacrifice and *upavitam* = thread, i.e., the thread consecrated by a sacrifice) in Sanskrit . It consists of three strands of cotton, each strand formed by three or nine threads. The cotton with which a thread is made, must be gathered from the plant by the hand of a Brahmin and carded and spun by persons of the same caste. It is hung on the left shoulder and falls on to the right hip. Out of the four varṇas, the Brahmins, Kshatriyas and Vaisyas are entitled to wear it. A child between the ages of 5 to 12 or 13 years is invested with the sacred thread when a ceremony is

performed. This gives the neophyte a right to appear before his preceptor to study the vedas and acquire knowledge. The triple cord symbolises, according to some authorities, (1) the three attributes of the deity, i.e., creation, preservation and destruction (Brahmā, Vishṇu and Śiva), and (2) body, mind and speech and the control over all of them. Footnote 1 on page 61 of *An Alphabetical List of the Feasts & Holidays of the Hindus and Muhammadans*, Superintendent, Government Printing, India, 1914.

3   Sanskrit *pu* = to purify and *nool* thread. Holy thread worn on the shoulders of the twice-born.

4   This forms Chapter XXI of *South Indian Shrines* by P.V. Jagadisa Ayyar.

5   This forms Chapter III of *South Indian Shrines* by P.V. Jagadisa Ayyar.

XVIII   Gayatri Japam

It is a scientifically proved fact that sound arranges the atmospheric atoms into definite shapes. Different sounds create different forms which continue to exist for a shorter or a longer period of time according to the strength of sound put forth to form them. The ancient sages knew this fact and made long and patient experiments in this direction and noted the effects produced by particular words known as *Mantras* or incantations. There is a separate science called *Mantra Śastra* dealing exclusively with this subject. One of these incantations goes by the name of Gayatri[1] Mantra and every Brahmin is bound to chant it a number of times at a sitting, repeating the process thrice everyday early in the morning, at noon and in the evening. The form created by the repetition of this Mantra[2] goes by the name Gayatri Devata.

As soon as a form as detailed above is created, it becomes a thing akin to our dynamo, wherein both human and divine energy is stored. The influence radiating from this form or Devata shields the individual from all malign and evil influences. If it is surcharged with sufficiently strong energy, it becomes in the hands of its originator a veritable angel ready to carry out even the slightest wish of its master.

Certain occasions are very favourable for creating these forms and surcharging them with energy. The occasion of solar and lunar eclipses are said to be specially favourable for this purpose. The people believe that the first day of the dark fortnight in the month of Avam (August-September) is highly conducive to the purpose of producing maximum effect with minimum effort. So this day is selected for Gayatri *Japa.*

The Gayatri Mantra is derived from the Rig Veda. The burden of the incantation is that the individual prays to the sun to give him light, knowledge, and energy. In fact he is in the midst of all these but a certain amount of will is essential to absorb and assimilate some of these energies of the sun and the repetition of Gayatri Mantra enables him to accomplish it successfully.

The posture most favourable for the easy assimilation of the sun's energies is supposed to be the one facing the sun in the morning when one chants the Gayatri Mantra. Before the commencement of this Japa (prayer) prāṇāyāma[3], or the control of breath and rythmic inspiration and expiration, is prescribed. This practice makes it easy for the individual to keep the mind centred on the understanding of the meaning of Gayatri Mantra more easily than it would otherwise be possible. This concentration strengthens the will and helps in absorbing and assimilating the solar energy and vitality. In fact, when the Gayatri Mantra is repeated, the sun is visualised in all his splendour radiating his energies everywhere especially on the practitioner. He should also think strongly with one pointed concentration that he is absorbing and assimilating the solar energy, becoming in his turn a miniature sun. By constant and continuous repetition of this practice he creates a centre of mighty force, himself remaining in the background as the source of that centre. The sun we see is in fact such a centre of force originating from a mighty consciousness remaining in the background.

The mechanical repetition of the words of the Mantra, without attempting to pierce through the veil of words and sucking as it were the sense contained in them, may not produce satisfactory results. To help in the process of keeping the wandering mind more or less fixed, careful counting of the number of repetitions is ordained.

If Gayatri Mantra is not repeated, keeping an account of the ingoing and outgoing breath is recommended to keep the mind concentrated.

People performing this Gayatri Japa, sit[4] in a pure and solitary place where distraction is not possible, and repeat the incantations[5], ten[6], twenty-eight or one hundred and eight times, as it suits their convenience. People should not practise this Japa with breaks and intervals. They should practise it every day during the whole of their lifetime. If there is a break, then they will make no steady progress but will only be marking time, remaining in the place they started from.

It is laid down that a rosary of twenty-seven, fifty-four and one hundred and eight beads may be made use of to keep in account the number of repetitions. The rosary may be either of *Rudraksham* or crystal beads. Counting on the fingers and on the joints of the fingers is also resorted to by many.

At the time of performing the Japa, the feet should not be pressing tightly against each other. The head should remain uncovered and the posture should be easy and convenient. In mornings, the hand should be placed near the navel, at midday near the heart, and in the evenings near the face. This action facilitates the storage of energy absorbed from the sun.

People performing Japas may sit on a piece of silk or blanket spread on the ground. The skin of a tiger, or a deer is said to be the most suitable thing to sit on and meditate. Mats made of durva grass and planks of all trees and of certain trees in particular, are also recommended as suitable. The āsanas (seats) used for this purpose should not be used by others if one wants to preserve the efficacy of the Japa. It is said that even the seats used by one practising the art of meditation are made pure and holy and consequently they should not be rendered impure and unholy by contact with unholy and impure persons or things.

The Gayatri Japa performed with the aim of helping the world and not with the aim of personal gain, is said to be a Yajna or sacrifice. The benefit resulting from the Gayatri Japa should be placed whole-heartedly and unreservedly at the disposal of humanity. Then the energy goes to the universal reservoir of such energies from which humanity as a whole is receiving help on suitable occasions to make progress. Temples and other places, where people gather in large numbers, are chosen for showering the energy stored in this reservoir by its guardian angels.

The sun according to his various functions is called by various names. He is called Nārāyaṇa in his preservative aspect. The eight Dikpālakas or guardian deities are, in reality, his outposts. In meditation, the sun should be conceived in the centre of a lotus flower of light petals representing the eight Dikpālakas. Indra symbolising the desire to do good should be located in the petal in the east. Agni representing sleep, laziness, etc., should be located in the petal in the south-east. Yama representing cruelty should be made to occupy the petal in the south. Niruthi representing sinful actions should be located on the petal in the south-west. Varuṇa, the symbolical representation of playfulness, should occupy the petal in the west: while Vāyu representing travel, adventure, etc., should occupy the petal in the north-west. Kubera represents sexual enjoyment and Isana represents the desire for wealth. These must be made to occupy the petals in the north and north-east respectively.

NOTES

1   The word Gayatri means 'that which saves when chanted.' It is therefore the Eternal sound, the word that was in the beginning, the Saviour. This sound pervades the whole universe, yes, it

creates, maintains and destroys it. These three aspects of the Logos — the Gayatri, the song, the saviour, are symbolised above. This is the highest meditation, hearing of this cosmic chant, the śruti, is the highest revelation. Meditating on the Gayatri leads us to aspire towards this goal. See Note on page 113 *Daily Practice of the Hindus*, Panini Office, Allahabad.

2   For directions see chapter XXII, pages 98 and 99 of *Daily Practice of the Hindus*, Panini Office, Allahabad.

3   This refers to the Regulation of Breathing, page 81 of *Daily Practice of the Hindus*, Panini Office, Allahabad

4   The *āsana* (seat) may be of a piece of silk spread on the ground, or a blanket, or a skin of antelope, or linen, or wood, or leaves, etc. No one else should use it. The bed, āsana, dress and drinking vessel should never be used by another — they are pure so long as they are used by one's own self. Page 99, *Daily Practice of the Hindus*, Panini Office, Allahabad

5   The number of incantations should always be counted; as those performed without keeping any count leads to a state of mental vacuity and passivity which is extremely undesirable. Countless Japa is therefore called asuric Japa. Page 98, *Daily Practice of the Hindus*, Panini Office, Allahabad.

6   The repetition 1,000 times is the best, 100 times is middling and ten times the lowest, at morning. In the evening 30 or 10 times. Page 99, *Daily Practice of the Hindus*, Panini Office, Allahabad.

XIX

Krishṇa Jayanti

Vishṇu, the preservative aspect of the universe and one of the Hindu Trinity, is said to take birth in this mortal world of ours whenever it is overburdened with evil-doers and sinners, who by their wicked actions upset the equilibrium of the earth. One such incarnation is his birth as the son of king Vasudeva and his wife Devaki Devi of bygone ages. He was then given the name of Sri Krishṇa, and his story is recorded in the famous work of the Hindus known as *Bhāgavatam.*

Born to rid the world of the wicked, he was secretly brought up by the chief of the Yadavas[1] (cowherds) to whom he was taken as soon as he was born, since his uncle Kansa considered him an enemy and wanted to get rid of him as soon as he was born, by putting him to death.

The birthday of this marvellous child is celebrated as a festive and sacred day on the eighth day of the dark fortnight in the month of Śravana called Avani in Tamil which corresponds to the English months of August-September.

The festive day is known by different names. Some call it Krishṇa Jayanti day. A few call it Janma Ashtami day, while a good many call it Gokula Ashtami and Sri Jayanti.

The myth relating to the advent of this mighty soul on earth is as sketched below:

The mother earth is said to have brought to the notice of god Vishṇu, that the population of the earth had enormously increased, that virtue was being trampled down by the tyrannical wicked and that she felt the burden rather unbearable. Vishṇu thereupon is said to have consented to rid the earth of the superfluous population by destroying the wicked. To accomplish this purpose, he took birth on this earth, as the son of a king who was under the persecution of his brother-in-law, Kansa, a veritable demon in human shape. But he had to be secretly brought up by others to avoid being put to death by his cruel uncle.

He is said to have accomplished the main object of his incarnation on this earth by having punished the wicked and helped the virtuous.

The *Dharma*[2] of each individual was fixed by him on a permanent basis, and proper arrangements were made for the protection and guidance of the world.

This avatar or incarnation of Vishṇu is said to be a typical one since he had combined in his divine personality the three aspects of creation, preservation and destruction to demonstrate to the world the oneness of the cosmic deity.

That he was a typical and ideal child is demonstrated by his boyish freaks and escapades described in prose and verse and read and sung over the length and breadth of the land by thousands of people.

His adventures with the *gopis*[3] and the manner in which he made one and all love him, shows that he was a youth of marvellous beauty and an ideal lover.

The destruction of the wicked and the masterly manner in which he conducted military operations shows that he was a warrior to the core, unparalleled in the annals of any history.

A wise counsellor he assuredly was, and it is demonstrated by the decision arrived at by the Pandavas under his instructions.

The teachings imparted by him to Arjuna on the battle field, graphically described in the famous work called *Bhāgavad Gita*, reveal him as the greatest philosopher of all ages and times, and a yogi of the highest order.

Though there are innumerable temples dedicated to Vishnu, the numbers dedicated to his incarnation as Sri Krishna are few and far between. The reason for this is perhaps that people have taken to worship him through paintings and not through temple images.

The various forms in which Sri Krishna is worshipped are, (1) the Bala Gopala Krishna or the baby Krishna, (2) the crawling Krishna or Krishna as a child on all fours, (3) Govardhana Uddhara Krishna or Krishna who lifted up the mountain, (4) Venugopala Krishna or the cowherd Krishna with the flute, (5) Kalingamardana Krishna or Krishna in the posture of dancing on the head of a serpent to punish the same for its wickedness and (6) Radha Krishna and Rukmani Krishna or Krishna in company with Radha and Rukmani.

In the great Mahabharata war, Sri Krishna acted as a charioteer to Arjuna, also called Pārtha. Hence he derived the name Pārthasārathy or the charioteer of Pārtha. A temple is dedicated to him in this aspect at Triplicane⁴ in Madras, known as Sri Pārthasārathy temple and it is one of the important temples in southern India.

There is also a temple dedicated to Sri Krishna in Conjeevaram⁵ and it goes by the name Pandavadhoothar temple or the temple of Krishna who went as a messenger of the Pandavas.

The temple in Mannargudi in the Tanjore district is known as Rajagopalaswami temple and it is dedicated to the memory of Vishnu's incarnation as Sri Krishna.

There are also temples of this god in the holy place called Udipi in the South Canara district and at Trivanjikolam near Iringalakuda on the Shoranur-Cochin railway line.

NOTES

1 The descendants of king Yadu. It is a caste title taken by the shepherd tribes.

2 Sanskrit *dhri* = to hold; that which is to be held fast; ordinance; charity; religious merit; justice. One of the four objects of existence; the other three being *Artham* = wealth, *Kamam* = pleasure and *Moksham* = absolution.

3 Sanskrit *gopi* = cowherdess.

4 This forms Chapter II of *South Indian Shrines* by P.V. Jagadisa Ayyar.

5 This forms Chapter I of *South Indian Shrines* by P.V. Jagadisa Ayyar.

XX

Ananta Vrata

The Hindu festival known as Ananta Vrata is observed on the fourteenth day of the bright fortnight in the month of Bhādrapada called Avani in Tamil, which corresponds to the English months of August-September. The observance of this Vrata is believed to secure for the observer immunity from all sorrows. Some men go to the extent of saying that even a lost situation may be regained by a faithful observance of this Vrata.

The festival is celebrated in honour of Lord Nārāyaṇa, the aspect of worship being one prior to the evolution of the worlds and the creation of the living beings.

The word *Ananta* means 'endless.' Therefore the Vrata called 'Ananta Vrata' is the worship of the deity who exists endlessly. In fact, time and space will cease to exist for one who raises himself to this state of consciousness.

The form in which the deity is worshipped on this occasion is one in which he reclines on the back of a hydra with śankha and chakra (conch-shell and wheel or discus, the usual appendages of Vishṇu) in his left and right hands respectively.

A serpent or hydra generally symbolises space as well as wisdom. A reclining posture represents the state of inactivity. Hence the form used for worship on this occasion rightly symbolises the period of inactivity called pralaya[1] or when the consciousness of the deity remains unmanifested. While he goes to sleep, everything goes to sleep following him. When he manifests himself, everything is manifested. At the time of pralaya, the various centres of consciousness, called jivas are said to be like particles of gold dust in a lump of wax, with the consciousness centred in themselves.

Aeons of ages are said to pass by between the commencement of a pralaya period and a period of activity. The period of inactivity is said to be a night for the deity and the long period of activity is a single day for him. When he awakes from his sleep, or in other words, when he begins his activity afresh and manifests his divine potentiality, he shoots a lotus bud out of his navel which blossoms into a flower. From the centre of the flower, the Lord of Creation, Brahmā appears and creates the universe.

The mythical incident referred to above is highly allegorical and it graphically describes the *Anda-Srishti* or the genesis of the cosmos. It deserves to be deeply pondered over.

Lord Nārāyaṇa, the aspect of the deity worshipped on this Ananta Vrata day, symbolises the spirit of God brooding over the waters of space or the primordial substances out of which future cosmos or universe arises because of the application of His will.

The seven-headed hydra on which Nārāyaṇa is said to rest, symbolises space and eternity, as has already been pointed out. The seven hoods or heads of the Śeshanāg stand for the seven forces, playing in the seven worlds of matter in the universe, kept under his domination. Some say that this hydra of Vishṇu has only five heads and not seven, deriving it perhaps from the Hindu philosophy which says that a man has only five *kosas*[2] or bodies, corresponding to the five kinds of matter in the universe commanded by five kinds of forces.

At any rate, as the hydra has only one body there is only one force and consequently only one kind of primordial substance. This force divides itself into seven or five, creating as many varieties of matter for the formation of the various universes of finer matter, pervading and interpenetrating the coarser ones near. Practical yoga consists in reducing the number of these forces playing in and around man and finally merging them into the one force of the cosmic deity in his first abode, and realising the state of consciousness he is in.

The tantric observances of this Vrata are very interesting and highly instructive. The observer of the Vrata ties round his right arm a cotton band formed of fourteen threads and going by the name 'Ananta Daram'. The expression conveys the idea of the feeling of the observer that he realises for the time being the forces brooding over matter without affecting it at all. Cotton threads are symbolical representations of lines of forces. Learned yogis say that the core within a nerve is a streak of light in a bed of space. The bed of space is the body of Brahma, which is beyond grasp. The conception of a form with only streaks of brilliant lines of light creating a luminous sphere, is the conception of the form of an angel and that of a man in his final ethereal body. Even plants and animals have a web of these lines of forces more or less brilliant, causing around them more or less luminous spheres.

The Ananta Daram or the string to be worn on the Ananta Vrata day, is first placed on a *chakra mandala* which is symbolical of health and wealth. At the end of the puja, it is taken out and worn on the right upper arm.

This aspect of the cosmic deity is worshipped on a day when the moon is in the asterism Mrigasira (orionis) in the month of Margasira, to shake off sterility and to get good children. The worship is given the name of Putra Ananta Vrata. If human will is centred for a sufficiently long period of time on the attainment of certain desired ends at particular hours or particular days considered favourable for particular purposes, successful results are sure to follow. A belief in this statement makes people observe some Vrata or the other to obtain the objects in view. In fact, the Hindus believed, believe, and will continue to believe that no attainment is impossible, provided sufficient will power is directed at the desired ends.

The chief forms of manifestation of Mahavishnu are four in number, and they are known as, Vāsudeva, Sankarshana or Adisesha, Pradyumna and Anirudha.

Vāsudeva is his consciousness in the highest and, perhaps, the finest form of matter.

Sankarshana is his conscious existence in the next level lower to the one mentioned above, and the other two are said to stand for his śankha and chakra.

Vishnu is always represented with four hands. In two of his hands, he holds nothing, having them ready to give his blessings. Of the other two which he raises, he holds in the right the chakra or the discus and in the left the śankha or the conch-shell. These two are symbolical to denote chastisement and punishment of the evil-doers.

The ten avatars[3] or incarnations of Vishnu are:

(1) Vārāha avatar: In this incarnation of Vishnu as a boar, he destroys an asura by name Hiranyaksha, to recover the earth from him, which was stolen by him and hidden under the ocean.

On the twelfth day in the bright fortnight of the month Magha, (January-February) which is known as Vārāha-Dvādasi, the anniversary of this boar incarnation is celebrated.

(2) Narasimha avatar: In this half man-half lion avatar or incarnation, Vishnu kills one Hiranya Kasipu, an asura, for blaspheming him, having come out of a pillar when challenged by the asura to do so. He shows, by this act of his, that he is omniscient and omnipresent.

The anniversary of this avatar is celebrated on the fourteenth day of the bright fortnight in the month of Vaisakha when the asterism Swati (*bootis*) is entered into by the moon.

After the destruction of Hiranya Kasipu, Narasimha did not abate his terrific nature. So the devas were considerably alarmed. In order to mitigate the fury of Narasimha, Iśwara is said to have assumed the Sarabha[4] form. People believe that the worship of this form would secure for them success over enemies in battles and immunity from diseases.

(3) Vāmana avatar: In this dwarf avatar, Lord Vishṇu is said to have humbled the pride of Mahabali, a king who had usurped even the kingdom of Indra, the god of the heavens, by his prowess. He begged of Bali three feet of ground as a gift, and when that was promised, he assumed a huge form known as Trivikrama form and measured the whole of the heavens by one foot and the whole earth by the second. For the third foot of land, he placed his mighty foot on the head of Bali and pushed him to the nether world. Bali's life was spared as he was not thoroughly bad.

The worship of Vāmana in the *lagna*[5] or hours of the day known as Vrichika lagna, on the twelfth day of the bright fortnight in the month of Bhādrapada is said to confer on the worshipper prosperity and success in all the undertakings. If the day happens to be a Sunday with the asterism Śravana (*aquitoe*) ruling over it, it is said to be specially favourable for the purpose.

(4) Paraśurama avatar: In this axe-bearing incaration Vishṇu is said to have extirpated the Kshatriya race of asuric origin and exercised sovereignty in Malabar.

(5) Rama avatar: In this arrow-bearing avatar or incarnation Vishṇu is said to have killed Rāvaṇa, the king of the Rakshasas of Ceylon or Lanka. The incidents relating to this are recorded in the famous Hindu epic *Ramayana* emphasising the moral dictum — Though vice triumphs in the beginning, virtue would in the end crush it down and prosper.

(6) Krishna avatar: The lovely sky-complexioned Krishna is said to have killed the vicious king Kansa who was his maternal uncle.

(7) Matsya avatar: In this incarnation as a fish, Vishnu is said to have destroyed an asura or demon who had stolen the four Vedas from Brahmā, the creator. Vishnu is said to have recovered these Vedas from the bottom of the ocean where they were hidden by the asura, and restored them to Brahmā, to his intense delight.

(8) Kurma avatar: This form of tortoise is said to have been used as a place of rest for the mountain Mandara, used as a churning rod by the devas and the asuras when they churned the ocean of milk to obtain nectar or Amrit from it, by drinking which one is said to become immortal.

The anniversary of this avatar or incarnation is celebrated on the Akshaya Tritiya day in the bright fortnight of the month Vaiśakha (April-May).

(9) Balarama avatar: This incarnation is said to be the dual aspect of the avatar of Vishnu as Sri Krishna of Dvaraka. Many asuras are said to have been destroyed by Vishnu in his incarnation as the elder brother of Krishna.

(10) Kalki avatar: This horse-faced incarnation is yet to take place at the end of the Kali Yuga.

Of the numerous temples famous for these various avatars of Vishnu, Srimushnam in the South Arcot district is famous for the avatar named Vārāha avatar, Singaperumalkoil near Chingleput and Simhachalam near Waltair are noted for the Narasimha or half man-half lion avatar.

Tirukkoilur in the South Arcot district is dedicated to Tiruvikrama avatar referred to in the incidents relating to Vāmana avatar.

The temple of Ananta Padmanabhaswami in Trivandrum is said to commemorate the Parasurama avatar.

The Pārthasarathy temple at Triplicane in the city of Madras commemorates the avatar of Vishnu as Sri Krishna.

Of the above named avatars that going by the name 'Rama avatar' is perhaps most familiar to the people since the country has many temples dedicated to it. Ramaswami temple in kumbakonam in the Tanjore district, where he is represented as seated to be crowned, is one of them.

NOTES

1 Dissolution. The end of a *kalpa* or destruction of the world. See pages 716 to 718 *Manual of the Administration of the Madras Presidency*. Vol.III, Government of Madras, 1893.

2 Sanskrit *kush* = to embrace. One of the five sheaths of the soul.

3 For detailed information see *South Indian Shrines* by P.V. Jagadisa Ayyar.

4 For details see *South Indian Shrines* by P.V. Jagadisa Ayyar.

5 Sanskrit *lag* = to adhere; contact; point of contact or intersection of two lines. The rising of a sign of the Zodiac above the horizon.

XXI   Vināyaka Chaturthi

The Hindu ceremony known as Vināyaka Chaturthi or Ganesh Chaturthi is of perennial interest to the Hindus all over India. It is a Vrata observed on the fourth day in the bright fortnight of the month of Bhādrapada called Avani in Tamil, corresponding to the English months of August-September. It is performed to obtain knowledge of things and success in all undertakings. There is not a Hindu ceremony but commences with a puja of this deity. The reason for this is obvious. Grit and strength of will are necessary for success in all undertakings. Intelligence also must play its part well. The trunk of this elephant-headed deity symbolises grit and strength of will and the head of the elephant symbolises wisdom, so by worshipping Vināyaka, one makes up his mind to use grit and strength of will, wisely, in the undertaking he is going to set his hands to.

The myth relating to the origin of this deity with an elephant's head and a protruding paunch is as follows:

Once upon a time, Lord Śiva, one of the Hindu Trinity, was out hunting with his *Ganas* or attendants. His consort Parvati was alone. She desired to take a bath, but there were no attendants to guard the entrance of the bathroom while she was in it. By her occult powers she created a guard and placed him at the entrance of the bathroom with strict orders not to let anyone inside.

Śiva returned home after a short while and wanted to enter into the bathroom where his consort Parvati was. He was prevented from doing so by the guard placed at the entrance by Parvati. Wild with rage at the audacity of the fellow, who dared to prevent him from entering a room in his own house, Śiva drew out his sword and cut off his head. An altercation ensued shortly afterwards between Śiva and Parvati over this affair and Śiva in the end promised to restore life to the guard whom he had killed in a fit of anger. He sent one of his men to bring him the head of the first animal he saw in the forest with its head facing north,[1] to be placed over the trunk of the guard slain by him since he could not find the original head.

The attendant returned with an elephant's head[2] which Śiva placed on the trunk, restored the guard to life, and made him the *pati* or the chief of his Gaṇas to compensate for the wrong inflicted on him by his hasty act. From this incident, he is said to have derived the name Gaṇadhipati, which means the chief of the attendants.

The goddess Parvati is said to have created this guard on the fourth day in the bright fortnight of the month of Bhādrapada in a particular year. So this day has been chosen for his worship every year as specially auspicious and important.

This deity is said to have assumed different forms for a variety of purposes. On one occasion, he is said to have assumed the form of a mad elephant and pursued the virgin Valli whom his brother Subrahmanya loved madly, to make her seek his brother's protection in terror, which resulted in her deep love for her protector and eventual marriage to him.

On another occasion, he is said to have assumed the form of a crow to upset a pot of holy water kept by the sage Agastya in his hermitage on the Sahya[3] mountain in Coorg. The holy river Cauvery is said to have taken her rise from this spot.

On one occasion, when a fit for mischief was on him, he is said to have assumed the form of a youth to ply his jokes and tricks in the abode of certain sages. Though he was caught and chained to a pillar there for his mischief in the beginning, the sages came to know subsequently who he really was, and

offered him gifts of a kind of sweetmeat called *modakam*.[4]
From that time onward, people began the practice of
preparing this special kind of sweetmeat for offering to
Vinayaka and distributing the same among the youngsters.

The use of hariali[5] grass for performing the worship of
their god is also said to be of special importance.

Once there is said to have lived an asura called Gajamukha.
He was very powerful and compelled Indra and the other
devas to knock on their foreheads with their knuckles and to
sit and stand alternately to show that they were submissive
to him. Vinayaka is said to have destroyed this asura and
consequently the devas did before him what they were
compelled to do by the asura. The people copied this practice
from the devas and it has now become the custom with the
Hindus of all classes, when worshipping Vinayaka.

Vinayaka is said to ride on a *Mushaka* or a mouse. Some
say that this is symbolic of his relation to agriculture. The
word 'Mushakam' is derived from a word which means 'thief.'
A mouse steals corn, and hence this deity is worshipped to
protect the corn from the field mouse, since all the rodents
are said to be under his control. Further the deity's protuberant
belly is said to represent the barn or the storehouse for grains
and his ears the *surpa* or the winnowing tray.

The tusk, the single one that he possesses, stands for the
piece of iron in a plough which turns over the furrow, and his
trunk stands for sheaths of corn. The name Surpakarna given
to the deity lends support to this statement that he symbolises
agricultural operations.

Ravana, the king of the Rakshasas, is said to have
performed severe penance invoking the blessings of Śiva and
obtained from him a lingam or phallic symbol. The devas did
not want this lingam to reach Lanka, and consequently made
representations to Vinayaka.

Vināyaka, thereupon, stood on the way by which Rāvaṇa was coming, in the guise of a Brahmin youth. By his occult powers, he created an immediate urge in Rāvaṇa to answer the call of nature. He therefore asked the youth to hold the lingam for him for a few minutes with strict injunction not to place it on the ground on any account, since he was told by Śiva that dire consequences would ensue if he happened to do so. The youth promised to hold it for a specified period of time, but said that he would place the lingam on the ground if Rāvaṇa did not return within that period. Rāvaṇa consented, but could not return within the specified period. The youth then placed it on the ground. The lingam immediately took root and became immovable having become fixed to the earth. The spot, which is in Maharashtra, thenceforth came to be known as Gokarṇa, a very famous Hindu religious centre.

When Rāvaṇa returned and found out the trick played by the youth which spoiled his project of installing the lingam in his capital to ensure its prosperity, he grew very angry and gave him a severe knock on the forehead, upon which, Vināyaka showed him his true form. Rāvaṇa thereupon begged his pardon for the mistake committed by him unwittingly. To atone for the sin of this act, he knocked himself on his forehead with his knuckles, which practice was forthwith copied by others to propitiate Vināyaka when performing his pooja.

There is a myth explaining the origin of the custom of breaking a number of coconuts before Vināyaka for attaining success in any undertaking.

On one occasion, Vināyaka had to enter the palace of the king of Benares to bless a bridal pair there. An asura called Kuta prevented him from entering by assuming the form of a big rock. Vinayaka caused a number of coconuts to be brought there by the king and his people, and had them broken on the rock. This not only broke it into pieces but also drove the asura out of it. People thereupon copied this practice of breaking coconuts in front of Vināyaka, to overcome hindrances and impediments in any undertaking and it has since become one of the customs of the Hindus.

The great epic *Mahabharata* of the Hindus is said to have been written by this deity to dictation by the sage Vyāsa, at a single stretch, on Mount Meru[6]. One of his tusks was broken and uses in place of a style and from this act, he is said to have won the name of *Eka Dantam* or deity with one tusk or tooth.

There are temples for Vināyaka everywhere in India and the Hindus worship him throughout the length and breadth of the land. But the shrines of special importance are those in the village of Tiruvalanjuli[7] near Kumbakonam, Tiruvidaimarudur in the Tanjore district, Tiruchengattangudi[8] near Nannilamin in the same district of Tanjore, and Trichinopoly[9] where on the summit of a rock commanding the town, stands a special shrine of this god.

At Tiruvalanjuli, his form is represented in white stone. Also a metal image, representing him with his two consorts Vani and Kamali, exists in the temple there.

In the temple at Tiruvidaimarudur, the image is placed very near the sanctum of the God, since he is said to have worshipped Śiva in that place.

At Tiruchengattangudi, and in the small shrine in the southern main street at Chidambaram, he is represented with ordinary human heads.

In the thousand-pillared mandapa at Chidambaram, there is a carving of this deity, on one of the pillars known as Navanita Ganapati or butter-eating Ganapati.

Heramba or Panchamukha (five-faced) Ganapati forms are found in the Neelayathakshi Amman temple at Negapatam and in the temple at Jambukeswaram. In the former place, the image is made of metal with a lion as its *vāhana* or vehicle, while in the latter, it is made of stone only without any vāhana.

"Rāvaṇa's[10] mother was in the habit of worshipping a lingam for ensuring prosperity for her son. But Indra took it stealthily away, out of spite, and threw it into the sea. Rāvaṇa's mother thereupon refused to take even a morsel of food as her devotions were interrupted. Rāvaṇa promised his mother that he would bring the chief Ātma lingam down from Kailash, and left for that mountain, the home of Śiva. There he performed the most severe austerities. He had a melodious voice and sang so well that Śiva was pleased at hearing his own praise in verse. The king of Ceylon chopped off his own head, made strings out of its skin, and with the harp prepared from those strings, played to the satisfaction of the God of Kailash, who asked him to name his desires. Rāvaṇa thereupon asked for the Ātma lingam and for a wife as beautiful as Uma herself. Śiva took out from his own heart the luminous Ātma lingam as bright as a crore of suns and handed it over to the demon, with the injunction that it should never be placed on the earth except where it had to be located for ever. Holding the gem in his hand, Rāvaṇa repeated his request for a beautiful wife — as charming as the goddess. Śiva replied that his wife Uma had no equal in beauty all over the universe, and therefore he could only offer her as she was. Infatuated, Rāvaṇa accepted her, blinded as he was by the unholy lust for the Mother of the Creation. He placed her on his shoulder, and walked off with the mother of the god of war, Skanda! He was going to the south. When he was seen taking away the Ātma lingam and the goddess, all the gods were alarmed. Her sons Gaṇesh, Skanda, and Virabhadra, as well as Nandikeshwara, were all astonished. They went to Śiva and complained how he could part with their mother.

Lord Śiva smiled, and added that her great champion Vishṇu, the Lord of Vaikunth, would release her. Bhavani, or Uma, also began praying. She was and is herself a great power, but when ordered by her husband to go, she, as a dutiful wife, would not disobey. She, therefore, invoked the help of Vishṇu. Lord Vishṇu appeared before Rāvaṇa in the guise of an old Brahmin and asked him where he got so charming a wife from. The demon replied that she was given to him by Sadāśiva, the Lord of Kailash, and elated with the praise, walked apace. `Do look at her,' said the *pseudo* Brahmin. Here the power of Vishṇu made him forget himself and he took her down to gaze at her beauteous face. But alas! the all-powerful goddess had turned herself into an old hag. Dirty, hideous, with frightful eyebrows, sunken cheeks, and toothless mouth she stood there — a horrid, repulsive figure! The Brahmin laughed a cynical, satanic laugh and chided: 'Oh Rāvaṇa, what a beauty, for a wife of the emperor of Ceylon!' Rāvaṇa felt humiliated and disgusted and left her on the spot. As soon as he turned away, Lord Vishṇu, the husband of the goddess of wealth, established her there as Mother Bhadra Kāli, where she still lives. The demon returned to Kailash and complained to Śiva for giving him such a dirty hag. 'Yes, you speak the truth, my friend,' said he, she is a witch, a bad lot. She pervades the 'innumerable universes,' and she is invincible, you cannot rule her. She is uncontrollable.' God Vishṇu then created a charming girl and assured Rāvaṇa that she would be born as Mandodari, the daughter of Māyāsura, that she would marry him and be a faithful wife. Rāvaṇa was satisfied at this assurance and proceeded with the journey still holding the Ātma lingam in his hand. But as soon as he came to the same spot where he had left Uma, he met Gaṇesh who was in the guise of a cowherd. The great god of success was

requested by the other gods to save the Ātma lingam, and that
was why he waylaid Rāvana. At this moment, Rāvana felt an
uncontrollable call of nature. So painful was it that he had to
request Ganesh to hold the lingam in his hand for a few
minutes. Ganesh said that he had to take care of his cows and
could not wait for long. He could only stay for an hour and
a half at the longest. 'Quite sufficient,' thought Rāvana and
went aside, but he could not return quickly. Half an hour
passed and the cowherd (Ganesh) shouted, 'Beware Rāvana,
one *ghanta*[11] has passed.' Another half an hour passed and
another warning from Ganesh followed. But Rāvana could not
move. He made signs. He made violent gestures begging him
to stay! It may be noted here that in India speech is prohibited
while answering the call of nature. The third ghanta, or half
an hour, passed and Ganesh shouted, 'Off I go, sir. My cows
have strayed. I cannot stay.' He then placed the lingam on the
earth. At this very juncture Rāvana felt free to move and ran
after the cowherd (Ganesh), but he was gone. He disappeared.
His cows also disappeared, but Rāvana just reached one of
them as she was sinking in the bowels of Mother Earth.[12] He
caught the beast by its ear, but the whole of its body went
inside. This ear now seen petrified or fossilised is the relic
that has given the spot its name Gokarna, or cow's ear, from
goor, gau, a cow, and *karna,* an ear. Associated with the name
of god Mahābaleshwar, or the all-powerful, it is called
Gokarna Mahābaleshwar, and the chief goddess of the place
is called Bhadrakāli. Rāvana, the king of demons, the ten-
headed and twenty-handed giant, tried his best to lift the
lingam up but it was eternally fixed. He who could shake
Mount Kailash with his powerful and plentiful arms, failed
to uproot it, and that is why it is called Mahābaleshwar, the
all-powerful god. He then turned once more to the ear of the

cow and tried to pull the beast out of the bowels of the earth, but he did not have the power. The ear of the cow, the lingam of Śiva, and goddess Bhadra Kāli, are all still there, as three-in-one. All the gods worship them. Rāvaṇa's mother and brothers had to come there to worship. Once Vibhishaṇa came to the temple unexpectedly, while a Brahmin named Hemadpant was worshipping the god. He got frightened at the sight of the giant and hid himself in the *nirmal*,[13] or waste-bin containing the rejected leaves of the bel tree (*Aegle marmelos*) dear to Śiva. Devout Vibhishaṇa bowed to the lingam, took a pinch of the bel leaves, and placed it in his turban. Poor Hemadpant was carried in that pinch unnoticed by the giant. He went to Ceylon and there learnt the script known as *Modi* or modified *Nagari*. He again hid himself in the turban of the giant and as soon as the latter returned to the temple to pay his homage to Mahābaleshwar he escaped. He had thus been able to import a new script into the Maratha-speaking territory. Such is the tradition, but the fact remains that Shivaji introduced it in government correspondence, through his secretary Chitnis Balaji Avaji. It is therefore known as *Chitnisi valan*. Gokarṇa Mahābaleshwar, the seat of Bhadrakāli, is reached from Bombay coasting steamers, and is visited by thousands of pilgrims who have faith in this Purāṇa. Many of them prefer it to all other seats of Kāli, owing, as is related above, to the fact of the entire goddess being present there."

"[14] Once upon a time while elephant-headed Gaṇesh was riding in his mouse and passing from Satyalok (Brahmā's abode) through Chandralok (the moon's abode) he fell down. The moon, who is very proud of his (the moon is a male in Indian mythology) good looks, laughed at him. Gaṇesh cursed him and said: 'Oh you sinner, Oh you antelope-shaped-nimbus-faced fellow! Those who look at your face hereafter shall be falsely accused of offences against the law.' This curse produced consternation all over the universe. The moon hid himself in a lotus-flower. When he could not be seen, gods, rishis, gandharvas — all were very sorry. Headed by Indra, they went to Brahmā for advice. He said that god Ganesh alone was able to remove the baneful influence of his curse, and advised them to appeal to him. Brihaspati, the preceptor of the gods, was then deputed to the moon, to direct him how he should propitiate god Ganesh. The moon did as he was instructed. Lord Ganesh was pleased, and appeared before him in all his glory attended by the eight goddesses of success (*ashtasiddhi*). The moon begged to be pardoned. He was asked to name the favour he sought. He naturally begged that the terrible curse be wiped off. Ganesh refused. He said he would give him anything but that. The gods interceded. Ganesh revoked the curse. He said: 'On the fourth day of the month of Bhādrapada (Ganesh day) those who will see you shall suffer from the curse in the course of the following year; there is no gainsaying that. But sin will not touch those who will bow unto thee on every second day of each month.' At the further importunities of the repentant moon, Ganesh directed thus: 'If by accident any one happened to see the moon on the special Ganesh day he should fast on the fourth day (*chaturthi*) of the second half of a month, and worship me, and worship the moon with his consort Rohini as soon as they rise above the horizon. He should give to a priest a gold image of myself. He shall, if he does so, be protected from calamities.'

"[15]The goddess Durga expressed her desire to her lord, Śiva, that she felt a craving for a baby to suckle. Śiva smiled and remarked 'Why? You are the mother of the whole

universe.' But she said that it was sad to miss the pleasure
of actually nursing a baby and demanded that at least Kartik,
his son, born in another way and kept aloof from her, should
be brought to her. He consented and left Kailash to bring him.
Durga was however so intent on having a baby that she made
a doll and was looking at it. Vishṇu, the protector, noticed it
and thought it a good opportunity to please her. He therefore
entered the doll and it came to life! When Śiva returned with
Kartik he found that his wife had already one child in her lap.
She explained what had happened. They were both overjoyed
and invited all the gods to have a look at the lovely baby.
Among the guests was Śani, or saturn, notorious for his evil
eye. As soon as he threw a glance at the baby its head dropped
off! Alas! everybody was distressed and all the gods were
alarmed! Durga began crying, and Śiva could not bear it. At
her request, he sent his Gaṇas, or attendants, to find the lost
head, but they failed! At last he directed that the head of any
creature sleeping with its head towards the north should be
chopped off and brought to him forthwith. An unfortunate
cow elephant was found in that inauspicious position. Its head
was severed and taken to Kailash. Śiva placed it on the
mutilated body of the doll which came to life again! But the
hideous, disproportionate figure of a man with the head of an
elephant, distressed Durga. In order to compensate for the
disfigurement, Śiva ordained that he should be appointed the
head of the Gaṇas, or attendants, and called Gaṇapati (*pati*-
chief) or Gaṇesh (*ish*-chief or head) and that in all pujas he
should be the first deity to be invoked. He further added that
one who invokes Gaṇesh at the beginning of an undertaking
shall have his efforts crowned with success, and bestowed the
title of Siddhidātā, 'the success giver,' on the boy. Gaṇesh thus
became the departmental deity of success."

NOTES

1 In consequence thereof arose the belief that it is not right to sleep with one's head placed northward. See footnote 2 on page 165 of *South Indian Gods and Goddesses*, Rao Bahadur H. Krishna Sastrigal, Government of Madras, 1916. It is interesting to note that a comparative study of religions reveals the fact that the characteristics of Vināyaka are attributed to *Janus* of the Latins.

2 "The elephant's head and also the rat are probably emblems of the prudence, sagacity and forethought which the Hindus attribute to this divinity." Du Bois, *op. cut*, p. 638, f. 1 on page 31 of *Hindu and Mahammadan Festivals*, John Murdoch, 1904.

3 Western Ghats.

4 A ball-like cake having a pyramid on the top with sweet inside and covered over with boiled rice flour.

5 [The Brahmins] make use of it [the durva grass] in all their ceremonies in the belief that it possesses the virtue of purifying everything. An annual feast instituted in honour of the sacred druva grass is celebrated on the 8th day of the moon in the month of Bhādra (September) and is called the Durva Ashtami. By offering the grass as a sacrifice on that day, immortality and blessedness for ten ancestors may be secured; and another result is that one's family increases and multiplies like the durva grass itself, which is one of the most prolific members of the vegetable kingdom. Du Bois, *op. cit*, pp. 658-9, f. 1 on page 27 of *Hindu and Mahammadan Festivals*, John Murdoch, 1904.

6 The Olympus of India. Proverbially it is the finest of all things. It forms the central point of *Jambudvipa* and is said to be 84,000 *yojanas* high. Geographically it appears to be the high land of Tartary, immediately to the north of the Himalayas. The earth is described as a lotus floating on the great deep, having seven petâls called *dvipas* or continents around it, centre being the Mount Meru, on the top of which the Ganges pours from heaven, page 39 of *Madras Archeological Dept.* (Annual Reports published by the Government of Madras).

7   This is treated in Chapter XIV of *South Indian Shrines* by P.V. Jagadisa Ayyar.

8   This is treated in Chapter XXII of *South Indian Shrines* by P.V. Jagadisa Ayyar.

9   This is treated in Chapter XXIV of *South Indian Shrines* by P.V. Jagadisa Ayyar.

10 Pages 13 to 16, *Hindu Holidays and Ceremonials*, Gupte, Thacker, Spink & Co., 1919.

11 Roughly 24 minutes (about 2½ ghantas make an hour).

12 Throughout India the belief in the sanctity of earth is universal. The dying man is laid on the earth, and so is the mother at the time of parturition, page 58 of *Hindu Holidays and Ceremonials*, Gupte, Thacker, Spink & Co., 1919.

13 The flowers, etc., removed from idols after worshipping.

14 Pages 25 & 26 of *Hindu Holidays and Ceremonials*, Gupte, Thacker, Spink & Co., 1919.

15 Pages 42 & 43 of *Hindu Holidays and Ceremonials*, Gupte, Thacker, Spink & Co., 1919.

XXII   Navarātri

Navarātri or the nine holy nights is a period of festivity observed by the Hindus for nine days or rather nights after sunset, in temples in the month of Purattasi corresponding to the English months of September-October, commencing on the first day in the bright fortnight of the month every year. The object or aim with which it is observed is said to be to propitiate the goddess symbolising every possible kind of energy in the universe, with a view to obtain perpetual happiness and prosperity.

Many of the greatest philosophers of the world are of the opinion that nature builds everything by 'forms and numbers.' Geometry is the science of forms and arithmetic is the science of numbers. The former may be said to be specially related to architecture while the latter makes order and limitation possible in the universe.

It is a very interesting fact to note that Devi worship, if at all it is to be effective, should be by means of *yantras* or geometrical figures engraved on metal plates, having the figures or numerical digits, or alphabets of words, arranged in a particular order.

Chakras[1] and yantras are two kinds of engravings on metal plates, the former consisting of angles and petal-like parts, and the latter of triangles alone, either single or in combination or interlacing in different ways. There is also another *pithas* said to be used in invoking the manifestation of the powers of the deity. These pithas are nothing but the clear-cut metal images of the deity, while meditating upon her.

The reason why nine days, and neither more nor less, are chosen as the duration for the observance of this festival is interesting and deserves examination.

The digit nine contains all the other numbers of one digit within it, but itself is not contained in any of them. So Devi or goddess contains within her the whole universe and no finite form can contain her as she is without any limitation. This fact is emphasised by the duration of nine days fixed for the observance of this festival.

The chief forms in which this goddess of the universe is worshipped are Kāli or Durga, Lakshmi and Saraswati.

Kāli or Durga is the wife of Śiva, representing the destructive aspect of the intelligence presiding over the universe, Lakshmi is the consort of Vishṇu, the preservative aspect, while Saraswati, the goddess of learning, is linked to Brahma, the creative aspect. Hence the three forces in the universe — the creative, the preservative and the destructive — are represented by these three forms referred to above.

It is believed by the Hindus that there are two aspects in the universe, namely, the positive aspect and the negative aspect. The positive aspect in creation, preservation and destruction is represented by the Hindu Trinity Brahma, Vishṇu and Rudra, while the negative aspect in these is represented and personified by the three goddesses referred to above, *viz.,* Saraswati, Lakshmi and Durga.

The personified Śakti in the destructive aspect of the universe is known by different names. In her mild aspect, she is worshipped as Uma or Parvati, the consort of Śiva. In her fearful aspect, she is worshipped as Durga, Kāli, Mahishasuramardini and so on. She derived the last name for having destroyed an asura named Mahishasura or asura in the guise of a he-buffalo. From this incident arose the custom of buffalo sacrifice to Durga by the lower caste Hindus.

People believe that the worship of the goddess Durga has been performed from time immemorial.

Her image, as generally visualised by the people for worship, is one of a ten-handed goddess. In one of her hands she is holding a spear with which she is piercing the giant Mahishasura. With one of the left, she is holding aloft the head of a giant. Her other hands hold different instruments of war.

A lion is leaning against her right leg and the asura with the buffalo head is leaning against her left leg.

The majestic deportment of the goddess with her ten arms and warlike attitude in which she is represented, combined with her sanguinary character, has made her the terror of all other gods. Her mighty exploits have given her an importance in the eyes of all the people not vouchsafed to any other deity.

Even the Hindu Trinity — Brahmā, Vishṇu and Śiva — are said to have done their best to propitiate her. Even Rama, son of Daśaratha and prince of Ayodhya, is said to have invoked her aid in his contest with the ten-headed giant Rāvaṇa, the king of Lanka, by worshipping her in the month of October. After this particular event, this puja came to be performed in the month of October, and not in any other month during the year.

As a refined taste is being cultivated, people have manifested a growing desire to decorate the image of the goddess going by the combined name of Durga-Lakshmi-Saraswati, with splendid tinsel and gewgaws to heighten the magnificence of the spectacle in popular estimation.

Families in affluent circumstances, rack their brains to find new and more gaudy embellishments for their images to outvie those of their neighbours in the magnificence of the decoration.

Certain classes of men, drawn chiefly from the lower strata of society, subsist solely on the income derived from trade in these tinsels, gewgaws and toys, made of clay or sawdust and beautifully and artistically coated with colours.

During the nine days of this Navarātri festival, toys in large numbers, tastefully decorated and arranged on galleries, are exhibited in almost all houses with the belief that the goddess is present in those toys and enjoys the worship offered to her. It is a pleasant sight to see young girls in their gaudy gala dresses and looking very smart and active going from house to house in the village in the evenings after sunset, to invite the maidens and girls of that village to their houses during the puja performance and to partake of the daily offerings to the goddess.

It is said in Hindu religious scriptures that heaven and every conceivable happiness are the results of sacrifices. Not understanding the principle implied in the word 'sacrifice' people took it for granted that animals were created for sacrifices. The people of bygone days thought that sacrifical offerings to certain bloodthirsty and carnivorous deities and feasting on the flesh of the slaughtered animals, really paved the way for salvation and celestial bliss. Hence even today sacrifices are supposed by some to result in the remission of the sacrificer's sin and in the blessings of the deity.

Thousands and thousands of oxen and sheep were and are slain every year before the altar of certain deities like the Durga Devi. In fact, it is said that large heaps of the flesh of the slaughtered animals had to be thrown away on many occasions for lack of men to eat them. In this connection, it may be added that a successful cutting off of the head of the animal at one stoke, meant good luck for the sacrificer. Such indeed is said to be the belief of a large number of Hindus belonging to the lower strata of the society, who offer animal sacrifices to the deities.

Another form in which this kind of manifested Śakti is worshipped goes by the name 'Kāli.' She is generally represented as standing on the breast of her lord Śiva with protruding tongue, having four arms, one holding a scimitar, another the head of a giant she had slain in fight, the third spread out as if bestowing blessings on her devotees, and the fourth as if she were welcoming the blessed. She is also represented as wearing a necklace of skulls and a girdle round her waist, formed of the hands of the giants she had slain. These horrid sights, combined with her dark figure and locks of hair hanging down to her heels, manifest the terrifying character of the goddess.

Why she is represented as standing on the breast of her husband Śiva is explained in the following incident.

On one occasion, she had gained victory over a formidable giant. Elated and intoxicated with joy, she is said to have commenced a frantic dance in the battlefield forgetting everything. The earth trembled, the gods were terrified and there was no peace on earth. No one dared to approach her when she was in such a temper. At last Śiva, her husband, was persuaded by the devas to go to her and pacify her. When he attempted to do so, she would not recognise him in her frenzy and so he had to throw himself among the corpses of the slain to remain there till recognised by her.

As she continued to dance, she inadvertently stepped on the breast of her husband, who taking the opportunity drew her attention to him by stirring and showing signs of life.

When the fit of frenzy had left her, she came to herself and stood aghast at what she had done.

She felt shocked and ashamed at the unhappy accident, and as a result of that feeling, bit her tongue having protruded it. From this incident she came to be worshipped by her followers, with Śiva under her foot and a protruding tongue.

Though the gross materialisation of the basic principle shocks one, the allegory of the observance is a significant one.

Śiva, as has already been shown, represents the destructive aspect and the manifestation of this aspect by him is Śakti. The destruction of forms is always a ghastly sight. Hence has arisen the custom of the observance of this ghastly form of propitiating the goddess, forgetting the basic principle conveyed by it, and basely abusing it by the materialistic tendency into which humanity is gradually plunging.

The higher class people of the Hindu society generally worship the preservative and the creative Śaktis only and they are known as Lakshmi and Saraswati. So the deities worshipped in their houses during the Navarātri days are Lakshmi and Saraswati. If at all the destructive Śakti is worshipped, it is only in her milder form, known as Gauri, Uma and Parvati.

The first day of this Navarātri festival, if it is ruled over by the asterism Hasta (*corvi*), is said to be specially suited for the Devi worship to invoke blessings on the whole world. The Vrata in which the goddess Gauri, represented as seated on a white elephant is worshipped, goes by the name 'Gaja Gauri Vrata.' This Vrata, observed at the hour when the sun enters the asterism Hasta, is believed to bring worldly prosperity for the observer.

An image of Gauri is made and worshipped on the first Tuesday in the month of Śravana. After the puja or worship is over, the image is gifted to a deserving Brahmin with money, pan-supari, flowers, fruits, etc., by women, to insure their immunity from widowhood and to give them good children. The observance of the Vrata, in this manner, is given the name of 'Mangala Gauri Vrata.'

A noteworthy feature in the observance of the Navarātri Vrata is that virgins, ranging from the age of two to ten, are offered gifts of saffron, vermilion flowers, sandal paste, fruits, etc., after the Gauri puja. The reason for this is obvious. Nine Śaktis or forces of Devi are recognised. These are personified and given the names of (1) Kumari, (2) Trimurti, (3) Kalyani, (4) Rohini, (5) Kalika, (6) Chandika, (7) Sambhavi, (8) Durga and (9) Subhadra.

Kumari represents the playful activities in babies making and,unmaking things. Devi's activity directed to the creation of Brahmā and the devas is akin to this play of children though at a higher level. Hence babies are given special treatment on the Navarātri days.

The Śakti named Trimurti is said to bestow good children; Kalyani education and royal friendship; Rohini freedom from sins; Chandika wealth; Sambhavi success in undertakings; Durga removal of impediments; and Subhadra desired objects. All these possibilities are there in virgins and consequently they are chosen for special treatment. It is said that in their selection, care must be taken to exclude the deformed, the slovenly, the bad-smelling, the sickly and the blind. Beautiful virgins, belonging to good families, should be chosen since they are to be considered as representations of Śakti who is perfect in everything.

The Navarātri festival is also known as the Dasahara festival. On the ninth and the last day of this period, the goddess Saraswati is worshipped. The worship is known as Saraswati Puja. It is interesting to note that this puja is performed in honour of the element *Vāyu* (air). The goddess is installed in a pot called *gadam.*

In ancient days when cudjan leaf manuscripts were in vogue, they were neatly arranged on a plank and the worship was offered to Saraswati, by worshipping those manuscripts. Nowadays, printed books, pens and pencils take the place of the cadjan leaves, manuscripts and styles.

If the Saraswati puja day happens to be a Tuesday or the day on which the moon is in the asterism Hasta, the occasion is said to be specially auspicious for her puja.

On the day during the festive period when the asterism Moolam is in the ascendency, Saraswati is installed on the books arranged for her worship; oblations and sacrifices are offered on the occasion of the next asterism Pooradam; and a happy send-off is given to her on the ensuing day when the asterism Tiruvonam (*Aquitoe*) holds sway.

The ceremony of installation goes by the name *avahana,* and that for sending her off is known as *visarjana.* The instilling of life in the image and the send-off given after the puja ceremony is over, are considered most religious and sacred, since the former action is akin to charging a dynamo with the mental force or electricity while the latter may be compared to the act of storing it away to be brought out for use on the next occasion when needed. There are potent incantations recited on both these occasions.

It is no doubt true that the Hindus worship idols and images. But when the basic principles, on which the avahana and visarjana referred to above are based, are taken into consideration, it will be seen that the images are intended to serve the purpose of a means to concentrate the mind on the abstract idea of a deity without material form, and that they are not ends in themselves.

The centre of force thus created, persists and may be attached to a fresh form or image if the original one is defaced or mutilated. But the newly formed image should be similar to the one replaced with its various parts having proportions in accordance with the dictates of *Śilpa Śastra* or the science of architecture. The mutilated and cast-off image should be thrown into deep water to avoid creation of mutilated thought forms in the minds of people, when they look at it.

The day next to the Mahānavami day on which puja to the goddess Saraswati is performed, is known as Vijaya Daśami. The word *vijaya* is the name given to the twilight hour between sunset and nightfall. This hour is said to be highly favourable for certain occult developments. The nature of this twilight has eluded the grasp of even very great men. Anyhow the word vijaya may be taken to mean auspicious and 'Vijaya Daśami' day may well be called 'a day of auspicious beginning.'

Tourists select this occasion for embarking on their journeys, and children begin to learn their alphabets for the first time on this occasion only.

If the Vijaya Daśami day happens to be presided over by the asterism Tiruvonam the occasion is said to be highly meritorious and auspicious.

A tree called the *vanni* (*Prosopis Spicigera*) is worshipped on this occasion for the reason that it once had given relief to Parvati by its shade when she was much fatigued. Sri Rama, hero of the *Ramayana*, is said to have circumambulated this tree in his rambles in search of Sita, to get her back. The Pandavas are said to have concealed their arms in a vanni tree when they had to lead their lives incognito.

The importance of the Vijaya Daśami day as an auspicious one, for the beginning of a new venture, is emphasised by the following myth:

Lord Śiva once went into a state of yoga trance called *nirvikalpa samādhi.* By this act of his, he controlled the play of forces in the senses. As his senses remained controlled, there was no play of such forces in the world and consequently there was no activity among men and certain classes of devas. The higher devas grew anxious and desired Manmatha, the god of all desires, to disturb Śiva's samādhi and bring him to the lower level of consciousness where the *indriyas* or sense-organs have full play. When he attempted to do so, Śiva opened his third eye of destruction and looked at Manmatha. This act of Śiva reduced Manmatha to ashes.

Śiva's first born Gaṇesa, in a playful mood, formed out of the ashes of Manmatha's body a mould which was subsequently filled with life by Śiva, and it then became a cruel demon named Bhandasura.

This demon performed severe penance and obtained from Śiva the boon that none but the Devi could destroy him. When it became imperative that he was to be destroyed in the interest of the universe, the Devi assumed different forms during the nine nights of Navaratri (since nights are asura's periods of activity while days are of devas') to destroy him but without success. On the tenth day, namely, Vijaya Daśami day, she prayed to that aspect in her Lord Śiva going by the name Kameśwara, and obtained from him the power to vanquish the demon and eventually to kill him. It is also said that by the union of this aspect of Śiva, Devi begot her second born Subramanya, the mighty teacher of gods and men.

As Rama began his march to rescue Sita from the hands of Rāvaṇa on this auspicious day, Hindu kings subsequently came to consider the day as one generally auspicious for starting on any expedition.

Nowadays, as there are no kings to conduct the expedition, in some states, grand Dasahara processions are arranged to keep alive the past memory and to impress on the people the importance of the occasion.

The other myths emphasising the importance of the observance of this Navaratri Vrata are given below:

In the golden age of bygone time, a king named Suketu lost his kingdom by the machinations of his relatives and had to take refuge in the forest with his wife. Covered with wounds, the king was being tended and consoled by his wife under a shady tree. The sage Angirasa chanced to come there, and taking pity on the unfortunate couple, advised the queen in exile to observe the Navarātri Vrata, by doing which, her husband was restored to health and reinstated in his kingdom. She is also said to have shaken off her sterility and given birth to a good child.

A pauper merchant named Suchela, in the kingdom of Kosala with a very large family to support, is said to have obtained plenty of wealth as a result of the observance of this Vrata.

Of the places specially sacred for the worship of Devi, the following are the most prominent: Conjeevaram[2] is said to be the place where Devi had once performed rigid penance. Madurai[3] is the place where she is said to have ruled with sceptre in her hand.

She is said to have danced with her Lord Śiva at a place called Tiruvalangadu near Madras, and acted the part of a midwife and nurse to a forlorn woman devotee of hers at Tirukkalavur near Papanasam in the Tanjore district.

At Mayavaram[4] in the Tanjore district and at Mylapore[5] in the city of Madras she is said to have worshipped Śiva having assumed the form of a *Mayura,* also called *Mayil* in Tamil, corresponding to the English word pea-hen, giving the places their respective names.

Tiruchengode[6] near Sankaridrug is famous as the place where she forms the left half of Iśwara's body.

NOTES

1 For detailed information on the subject, see page 185, *South Indian Gods and Goddesses*, Rao Bahadur H. Krishna Sastrigal, Government of Madras, 1916.

2 This is dealt with in Chapter II of *South Indian Shrines* by P.V. Jagadisa Ayyar.

3 This is dealt with in Chapter XXIX of *South Indian Shrines* by P.V. Jagadisa Ayyar.

4 This is dealt with in Chapter X of *South Indian Shrines* by P.V. Jagadisa Ayyar.

5 This is dealt with in Chapter I of *South Indian Shrines* by P.V. Jagadisa Ayyar.

6 This is dealt with in Chapter XXXXIII of *South Indian Shrines* by P.V. Jagadisa Ayyar.

The festival going by the name of Skanda Sashthi is observed on the sixth day of the bright fortnight in the month of Arpisi corresponding to the English months of October-November. The observance is to propitiate lord Subramanya, the second son of Śiva, in his aspect of Kameśwara for having overcome and destroyed the asura called Surapadma and his followers. The mythical incident relating to this is as follows:

Once the asuras had obtained from Lord Śiva innumerable boons. Puffed with pride at their achievements they had become arrogant, and one among them named Daksha had even gone to the extent of wantonly insulting Śiva by withholding his portion of the sacrifical offering (*yajnabhaga*) on a particular occasion.

In former times, there were different grades of beings known by different names such as Rishis, Deva Rishis, Brahma Rishis, Bhagavan, Devas and Prajapatis. The Daksha referred to above belonged to the order of Prajapatis and hence he was also styled Daksha Prajapati.

This Daksha Prajapati had a daughter named Sati, and Śiva desired very much to marry her. The feeling of love was reciprocated and Śiva and Sati were married. Shortly after, Daksha performed a sacrifice, but did not invite his son-in-law for it, nor did he offer him the portion of the sacrificial offering which was his due being one of the Trinity. Śiva of course resented the insult and the sacrifice was spoiled.

By the wanton insult offered to Śiva by Daksha Prajapati he had become a great sinner. Sati, filled with grief at the feud between her father and her husband, destroyed herself, but was born again as Parvati and married Śiva again.

At this time an asura named Taraka was harassing the devas. Unable to withstand his prowess the army of the devas broke and fled, and Indra, the celestial king, approached Brahma for advice. He directed him to use Manmatha's powers to rouse the love for Parvati, dormant in Śiva bent on yoga practice. By doing this he succeeded in making Śiva beget his second son Subrahmanya, who in course of time became the commander-in-chief of the army of devas and destroyed the asura Taraka along with his followers.

The mythical incident of the birth of Lord Subrahmanya with six faces, a dozen arms and two feet, is highly allegorical, interesting and instructive, full of spiritual and philosophical significance worthy to be deeply pondered over to get at the real significance of the myth. The myth itself, in brief, is as follows:

While Śiva was seated with his consort Parvati on his lap, the devas approached him and made representations that the asura Surapadma with his hosts of followers was harassing the devas and injuring the world. Roused to anger by these words of the devas, he emitted from the third eye on his forehead, six sparks of fire of surpassing brilliance and splendour.

Unable to bear the pulsating vibrations and radiance emanating from these sparks of mighty potency, the devas again prayed to Śiva to reduce the force emanating from them and make it bearable for them. He thereupon directed Vāyu, the god of wind, and Agni, the god of fire, to help the devas by using their powers to moderate the energy of the sparks.

By the influence of Agni and Vāyu the sparks having been reduced to smiling and shining streaks of splendour, were

wafted away to the fountain source of the holy river Ganges
on the mountain tops of the sacred Himalayan ranges.

After contact with the holy waters of the Ganges, these
gem-like sparks of fire gathered together in a bush of reeds
that was near, and assumed the form of a glorious being of
light and colour of dazzling brilliance and splendour with six
faces and twelve hands. Thus is described the origin of the
lord Subramanya of the Hindus.

Filled with wonder and admiration, the devas and others
fell to praising this second-born son of Iśwara, destined to
become not only the saviour of the world but also the teacher
of gods and men in this solar system.

It is interesting to note that Vishṇu, the preserver of the
universe, is said to have directed the Kritika dames (*Pleiades*)
to nurse this marvellous child and from this incident, he is
said to have derived the name Kārtikeya.

On one occasion, Brahmā, the lord of creation, is said to
have been challenged by Subrahmanya to expound the sacred
word *Praṇava*[1] to his satisfaction, and when he failed to do
so, he was imprisoned by our Lord in a cave. On Śiva's
interference, Brahmā was released, and Subrahmanya is said
to have thoroughly grasped the expoundings of Praṇava given
to Parvati by Śiva, even when he was an infant resting on the
lap of Parvati. It is therefore no wonder that he is recognised
by all as the lord of wisdom, a fact which is represented
symbolically by associating him with serpent, which stands
for space as well as wisdom according to circumstances.

A peculiar form of propitiating this deity is that of carrying
a *kavadi*[2] to any one of his temples, by a devotee from his
village or residence. This custom is rather unique and
deserves special attention and thought to reveal the mystery
behind the custom. At any rate, there is an allegorical myth
connected with the origin of the custom.

In Hindu scriptures, there is a mention made of a dwarf sage Agastya[3], who is said to have drunk the oceans dry on a particular occasion! Agastya is said to have been given two hillocks on Mount Kailash, the abode of Śiva in the north, with the permission to take them south to be located somewhere there and worshipped as Śiva and Śakti, spirit and matter. As the hillocks could not be forthwith removed, the sage returned to his abode known as Podiamalai, leaving the hillocks in a forest called Burchavanam. There he met an asura named Idumban, the sole survivor of the asura class, destroyed by the prowess of Subrahmanya, and who was in fact the preceptor of the asuras when they were in affluent circumstances. He begged the sage Agastya to accept him as his disciple and to initiate him in the mystery of the divine wisdom. Complying with his request, the sage directed him to go and bring the two hillocks left in the Burchavanam in the north to be located in the south. He also invested him with certain powers by which he was able to command the rod of Brahma and the services of the eight serpents — Vāsuki, Anantan, Taksha, Sangapalan, Gulikan, Padman, Mahapadman and Karkotakan, to remove the hillocks and carry them on his shoulders.

Using the huge and mighty serpents as ropes, he tied the two hillocks to the two ends of the rod of Brahma and was proceeding south carrying them, balancing them all on his shoulders. When he came to the place called Palni, Idumban felt tired and having placed the burden down, began to take some rest. Having recovered from the fatigues of the journey he tried to lift the burden from the ground to proceed on the journey, but to his surprise and dismay, he found one of the hillocks rooted to the earth, and do what he might he was not able to lift it! Mounting on top of one of them, he espied Subramanya there in the guise of a youth in underwear with a stick in his hand.

An altercation ensued between our Lord and Idumban which resulted in the latter's falling down on the ground senseless. Idumban's wife subsequently prayed to Subrahmanya to spare her husband, pardon him and bless him, who taking pity on the devoted wife of Idumban, restored him to consciousness and took him into his favour by making him his (*dvārapalaka*) gatekeeper.

From the incident referred to above, has originated the custom of kavadi-bearing by the Hindus to propitiate Subrahmanya.

There are many temples dedicated to Subrahmanya in southern India. The specially important places for the worship of subrahmanya are Tiruchendur[4] as the place where he was first worshipped for having destroyed the asura Surapadma; Tirupparankunram[5] near Madurai where he is said to have married a damsel by name Devasenai; Palni[6] near Dindigul where he appeared to Idumban in the guise of a youth; and Swamimalai[7] near Kumbakonam where he is said to have initiated Iśwara himself in the mysteries of Praṇava.

At Vaithiswarankoil,[8] he is worshipped as a lovely youth who is said to have obtained his *Velayutham* (invincible lance) from the goddess Śakti, and at Trichengode, he is worshipped in the form of a serpent.

Tirutani near Madras, is also important as the place where he is said to have married Valli, and a place called Kambankollai (not yet identified!) is made mention of, where he made Vināyaka threaten his lady-love Valli in the guise of an elephant to make her voluntarily fall into his arms and eventually wed him.

NOTES

1 From Sanskrit *pranu* = to utter. The Mystical syllable *om*.

2 From Tamil *kavu* = to carry on the shoulder and *tadi* = pole. Pole for carrying burdens, resting on the shoulder. This is here applied to the religious performance of a vow and in this case to the ends of the pole, pots filled with milk or sugar, are attached according to the vow taken. For further particulars see *South Indian Shrines* by P.V. Jagadisa Ayyar.

3 The life of this sage and his figure appear on *South Indian Shrines* by P.V. Jagadisa Ayyar.

4 This is dealt with in Chapter XXXII of *South Indian Shrines* by P.V. Jagadisa Ayyar.

5 This is dealt with in *South Indian Shrines* by P.V. Jagadisa Ayyar.

6 This is dealt with in Chapter XXVIII of *South Indian Shrines* by P.V. Jagadisa Ayyar.

7 This is dealt with in *South Indian Shrines* by P.V. Jagadisa Ayyar.

8 This is dealt with in Chapter VIII of *South Indian Shrines* by P.V. Jagadisa Ayyar.

XXIV   Deepavali Pandigai

Deepavali Pandigai goes by another name Naraka Chaturdasi Snānam, perhaps from a bath taken before daybreak on the fourteenth day of the dark fortnight in the month of Arpisi, corresponding to the English months of September-October. An asura named Narakasura is said to have been destroyed by Sri Krishṇa on this day and the festival is intended to commemorate the incident.

The word 'Deepavali' means a row of lamps and it originated perhaps from the custom of illuminating villages on this festive occasion. In course of time this was replaced, either wholly or partly, by fireworks. Children and even adults light firecrackers during the short hours before daybreak and enjoy it immensely. New clothes, and firework display are considered signs of auspiciousness and hence people wear new clothes after the auspicious bath and enjoy the occasion as set forth above.

The new moon day which immediately follows the Deepavali day goes by the name of Deepavali Amavāsyā day. The occasion is considered to be specially favourable to propitiate the manes (Pitris) of the departed and hence libations of water with sesame or gingelly seeds are offered to them with the necessary Mantras or chantings. This offering, performed by the fatherless on all new moon days, goes by the name *Pitri Tarpanam* which means an 'action to satisfy the manes of the forefathers.' The Hindus are enjoined to offer oblations of water everyday to satisfy the devas, the rishis (sages) and the Pitris (manes of the departed), and the new moon days are special occasions for the offerings to the manes of the departed. Certain new moon days are considered more suitable and more favourable for the offerings than other new moon days, and this new moon day is considered one such occasion. So people perform the *tarpanam* with special care and attention on this day.

There is a belief among the Hindus that there is a great reservoir of spiritual force in the universe in the custody of the Adhikarika Purushas or highly evolved souls who are responsible for the spiritual progress of human beings. These liberate portions of this force from the reservoir and pour them among the masses when they gather in particular places on particular occasions. Further, when the magnetic conditions are favourable, certain substances absorb the forces liberated and retain the property for a limited period. Gingelly[1] seed (*Sesamum Indicum*) is a favourite seed of the planet Saturn or Śani. Perhaps on the occasion of the Deepavali morning, owing to the peculiar position of the several planets, the Saturn is capable of charging the essence of his favourite seed, the gingelly, with special properties. So anointing the head with this oil on the occasion is considered to bestow on men and women, health, wealth and prosperity, in addition to spiritual progress. Further, water everywhere is believed to be saturated with holy magnetism on this occasion. Hence people think that water used for bathing in the early hours of the morning before sunrise is equal in merit to that of the Ganges which is always surcharged with the properties of very valuable herbs and with the magnetism of the great sages believed to live near the source of the sacred river and bathe in her sacred waters everyday before sunrise. When people meet one another after the holy bath, they ask one another whether they had the 'Ganga Snanam' or the bath in the waters of the Ganges. A special noteworthy feature on this occasion is that gifts of fruit, pan-supari, sandal paste, and even money are freely made to people going to visit friends, relations and even utter strangers. This custom is observed by people when bathing in the waters of the sacred rivers, without which a bath is not considered to be efficacious at all. Hence we find that the comparison of ordinary water with that of the Ganges is sustained.

The myth deriving the epithet 'Naraka Chaturdasi' is interesting.

Once there was an asura king named Narakasura, ruling over the universe residing at a part of the present Bengal Presidency. Though a great devotee of Vishnu, his rule was considered undesirable and consequently Sri Krishna was approached by the people. The lord proceeded to the place and overcame him on this day which, as the day of joy, was commemorated. King Bali, the weighty king of the asuras, began to usurp the kingdom of India. On being appealed to by Indra, god Vishnu, one of the Hindu Trinity, in the guise of a Brahmin dwarf, begged of the asura three feet of ground from his vast empire. When that was granted, Vishnu assumed a huge form going by the name 'Trivikrama avatara' and measured the earth and the heavens as two feet, and for the third, placed his foot on the asura's[2] head and pushed him down into the nether world. As he was a deep devotee and a being of great merit, Vishnu had to bless him with certain boons. To commemorate the advent of Vishnu as the dwarf (Vāmana) avatara and the giant (Trivikrama) avatara (incarnation), this occasion came to be considered as auspicious. Because of the boons conferred on the asura by Vishnu, the merits resulting from actions such as charity to the undeserving, sacrifices of clarified butter not poured in flames, *Sraddhas* (ceremonies) performed to satisfy the manes of the departed without observing the prescribed rites, and yajnas or sacrifices performed unaccompanied by the necessary gifts, go to king Bali.[3]

As king Bali is supposed to rule over the nether world, people do not like the idea of the merits of their action, not properly performed, going over to him and strengthening his power. So they are very careful to observe the rites and ceremonies, paying due attention to the formalities to be gone through in each case.

There is a strong belief current among the Hindus, that a beginning made on the auspicious Deepavali day will be conducive to prosperity and success. Hence the Vaisyas or the Hindu trading castes of northern and western India open fresh accounts every year on this day, after having performed puja to the goddess Lakshmi and distributed presents and gifts to those invited. They keep awake the whole night trying their luck in the game of dice. Even visitors are free to bet with, or play against one or the other of the persons engaged in the game with a view to try their luck. People walk miles with bags of money to be utilised in betting, and thus trying their luck when rich Marwaris and others are engaged in the game of dice. Large sums are lost or won, on the day in question, both by men and women of the Vaisya community, especially of the Bombay Presidency and of northern India. Even onlookers are given gifts every now and then by the winners from their winnings and there are also gift boxes for some charity or the other into which small sums are dropped every now and then by one or the other winner.

Speculative purchases and sales, which are nothing but forms of gambling on a gigantic scale, are resorted to by the wealthy merchants in certain parts of India, during the Deepavali week and especially on the Deepavali day and night.

NOTES

1   Sanskrit tila; *til* = to anoint.
2   See *South Indian Shrines* by P.V. Jagadisa Ayyar.
3   The *Mahabharata* gives the following legend about king Bali. It
    came to pass that Bali, the mighty king of the asuras, conquered
    Indra and the gods, and the gods came to the hermitage of
    Viśvamitra and prayed to Vishṇu for succour; and Vishṇu was
    re-born on earth in the form of a dwarf (Vāmana avatara),and
    he assumed the dress of a mendicant and went to the abode of
    Bali and asked the latter to give him as much earth as he could
    measure in three steps; and Bali granted his request. Then Vishṇu
    took a mighty form and took three steps; and the first step
    covered the earth; the second covered the heavens; and the third
    was placed on the head of Bali. Vishṇu then sent Bali and all
    his legions to the realms below the earth and once more restored
    the universe to the rule of Indra. (The Bhāgavata says that
    Vishṇu, out of love for his devotee Bali, took away his kingdom,
    in the shape of a gift, so as to enable him (i) to devote his whole
    soul to god alone; because with his kingdom went away all the
    cares and vanity attached to kingship; and (ii) to enhance his
    reputation for charity. Footnote 1 on page 28 of *An Alphabetical
    List of the Feasts & Holidays of the Hindus and Muhammadans*,
    Superintendent, Government Printing, India,1914.

The Hindu festival going by the name Kartikai is celebrated on the full moon day in the month of the same name corresponding to the English months of October-November, when the moon is in conjunction with the asterism Kritikai (*Pleiades.*)

Though the observance of the Vrata is to propitiate the five elements, greater importance is attached to the propitiation of Agni (fire) and all the houses are profusely lighted and illuminated after sunset, in consequence.

The reason why fire is given prominence over the other elements is furnished in the allegorical and deeply spiritual myth in which Lord Śiva, one of the Hindu Trinity, is said to have appeared in the form of a pillar of fire to teach the creative and preservative aspects, Brahmā and Vishṇu, the knowledge of infinity, beyond time, space and limit, on this particular occasion.

Brahmā is said to have assumed the form of a swan and flown upwards to find the top of the pillar, while Vishṇu took the form of a boar to dig down and reach its bottom. The flag-staff or *dhwaja-stambha* in temples, is intended to symbolise this pillar of fire. The Indian yogis (sages) say that the pillar of fire is nothing but the halo of brilliant light surrounding and interpenetrating the spinal chord within the spinal column in man.

The peculiar custom of burning heaps of dry leaves, twigs, etc., going by the name of *chokkappanai* in front of temples deserves its rational explanation. The custom appears to have originated from the incidents recorded in the myth wherein

Śiva is said to have burnt the chariots of certain asuras who were harassing the sages and others on this earth, at a particular period. The chokkappanai (the collection of dry leaves, twigs, etc.) is symbolical of the aerial vehicles of the asuras, burnt by the fire emanating from the third eye of Śiva.

There are a number of myths emphasising the importance of the observance of this Vrata. King Bali is said to have observed this Vrata to get rid of a burning sensation all over his body and the goddess Parvati herself is said to have observed it to be freed from certain sins she had committed, to wit, the breaking of a Śivalingam unwittingly, while engaged in single combat with the asura Mahishasura whom she slew.

A preparation of fried rice is considered specially acceptable to lord Śiva, and, the custom appears to have originated from the incident narrated in the Maha Bali myth, quoted above. Bali is said to have offered this preparation to Śiva to be freed from the burning sensation he felt in every cell of his bodily tissues, so to say.

The material, fried rice, is perhaps meant to symbolise the condition of the cells in the body of Bali that were being fried and consumed by the invisible fire. Its offering is intended to convey to Śiva the condition of the cells in his body and thus silently to beg for his mercy. Further, Bali perhaps thought that fried rice, when consumed by him, might not build cells causing the burning sensation since they are already subjected to fire by the frying process. Even though the burning sensation might not be altogether removoed by this diet, yet it might perhaps lessen the severity of the feeling, by forming cells incapable of furnishing as much burning matter as cells formed by the cells of cooked rice, raw rice and so on. These customs are symbolical and figurative and consequently, the idea conveyed must be taken in a restricted application of the language whose meaning should not be stretched. Śiva represents fire as he is the lord of the burning ground. So anything deprived of humidity and subjected to heat, might naturally be taken by people as an acceptable offering to Śiva. Hence, perhaps, arose this custom of offering fried rice to the deity on this occasion.

When temples are located on hills, they are considered to be specially suitable for worship and highly influence-radiating. As the temple at Tiruvannamalai[1] in the South Arcot district is one of such temples dedicated to Śiva, this festival is observed there with great éclat and thousands of people flock there every year, to witness the celebration, take part in them, and derive the blessings of the presiding deity Arunachaleswara.

The whole rock is illuminated and a huge flame of torch is lighted at its top after sunset on this festive day.

The hill consists of three fortified peaks. The isolated Tiruvannamalai peak is covered with jungles and is accessible only on foot. A natural column rises from the top of the hill perpendicularly, which the devotees of Śiva hold to be a lingam or phallic symbol. In fact this place is one of the five main Śiva centres in India, and, it is the abode of one of the five lingams brought from the highest of the super-physical regions, to wit Kailash, by Sri Śankaracharya.

This temple is considered by the devotees of Śiva to be as sacred as Srirangam is for the devotees of Vishnu.

The other important places for the observance of this Vrata are Tiruchengodu,[2] Palani,[3] Vedaranyam[4] and Tiruchendur.[5]

On the north wall of the central shrine in the Kalahastisvara temple at Kalahasti,[6] there is a record relating to the 12th year of the Chola king, Rajendra Choladeva I (1011-43 A.D.) mentioning a gift of gold for celebrating the festival of Kritika-dipa.

On the west wall of the first prakara of Brihadamba temple at Devikapuram,[7] there is an inscription of the Vijianagara king, Virapratapa Krishnadeva Maharaya dated, Saka 1443 *Vikrama,* Kartikai, Ekadasi, Monday, corresponding to 9th July 1920, which mentions providing ghee for lamps during the festival of Tirukartigai.

NOTES

1 This place is fully described in Chapter VI of *South Indian Shrines* by P.V. Jagadisa Ayyar.

2 This is fully described in chapter XXXIII of *South Indian Shrines* by P.V. Jagadisa Ayyar.

3 This is fully described in chapter XXVIII of *South Indian Shrines* by P.V. Jagadisa Ayyar.

4 This is fully described in chapter XXI of *South Indian Shrines* by P.V. Jagadisa Ayyar.

5 This is fuly described in chapter XXXII of *South Indian Shrines* by P.V. Jagadisa Ayyar.

6 This is numbered as No. 291 to 1904 *Madras Epigraphical Department* (Annual Reports published by the Government of Madras).

7 This is numbered as No. 361 of 1912 *Madras Epigraphical Department* (Annual Reports published by the Government of Madras).

XXVI   Arudra

The Hindu Arudra festival is observed in the month of Margasira also called Margali, corresponding to the English months of December-January, when the asterism Arudra (*orionis*) holds sway. The occasion is one specially favourable to propitiate the dancing aspect of Śiva (Nataraja), by worshipping him.

The asterism going by the name Arudra has for its presiding deity Rudra, symbolising an aspect of the destructive force in the universe.

The constellation going by the name Orion, has in its north-east corner, the asterism Arudra under reference. The constellations, planets, etc., are macrocosmic centres through which forces are poured out into this solar system for the evolution of microcosmic intelligences including men and the devas. Every conscious entity in the system has a microcosmic centre. In fact there are indissoluble links of magnetic forces connecting the macrocosmic and the microcosmic centres. For the purification of men's bodies, a certain amount of will power is necessary to emphasise the flow of forces from the macrocosmic centres through the microcosmic ones. Hence the worship of the deities presiding over constellations and asterisms is intented mainly to serve this purpose.

Certain planets and constellations can emphasise various kinds of emotions in men and certain asterisms can influence mental and spiritual aspects. The asterism Arudra in the constellation Orion can pour such magnetic forces into men's bodies, that will burn all dross and retain only pure gold —

gold taken in its highest sense of unsullied light. Hence worship of Rudra on this occasion is considered to be specially favourable for purifying lower and coarser emotions, in men.

There is a mystical allegory regarding the dancing aspect of Śiva. The key for the understanding of the hidden meaning conveyed by the allegorical myth lies in the word 'dancing.' It stands for the expression 'vibration.' We all know that intense vibration shakes off impurities and makes objects highly luminous and brilliant.

The myth says that Śiva danced before the sages and others to show his superiority. The sages and others are said to have directed against him various obstructing elements symbolised by serpents, etc. Śiva remained unaffected. He wore on his body certain forces symbolised in the myth, and trampled some under his feet. This portion of the allegory means that he shook away from him, the unassimilable forces and refined what could be refined out of the grosser forces.

It is also interesting to note that Śiva, on this occasion, is said to have assumed the guise of a beggar, aided by Vishṇu in the guise of a ravishingly beautiful woman, to teach the sages and their wives a lesson. Here also the meaning is clear. The word 'beggar' stands figuratively for the pure light divested of all garments of impurities. The enchanting damsel stands for the indescribably beautiful and brilliant form of light of Śiva's body, when cleared of dross adhering to it in the form of passions, emotions, anger, lust and so forth. In this connection, the expression 'Naked Christ should be followed by naked disciples only,' may be brought to mind. The incident in the story of the gopis coming to Sri Krishṇa naked to receive the garments they have to wear thenceforth, is also highly allegorical. It means that the gopis should be purified of all grosser feelings and emotions to wear his garment, namely, the body of light.

The story of the pariah Nanda[1] who is said to have passed through fire and merged into the body of Nataraja in the Chidambaram temple as a mass of light, emphasises what is set forth above. The story itself, in brief, is as follows:

In a village named Adhanur, there was a wealthy Brahmin, who had a faithful and honest pariah servant named Nanda for cultivating his land. This servant was seized with an ardent desire to visit the temple of Nataraja at Chidambaram and pay his humble homage to the deity there. As he was a pariah of the lowest caste, the Brahmin ridiculed the idea of his going to Chidambaram to worship Nataraja, considered inaccessible even to the great saints like Sanka, Sanatana and so forth. Finally, to get rid of his importunities, the Brahmin gave him permission to go, after having finished the work of cultivation of his vast lands, thinking that Arudra in the month of Margali, would have passed, long before he even finished a small fraction of the work assigned to him. But a miracle was performed for Nanda by Nataraja, and the work of cultivation of the Brahmin's field was finished in a single night without any defect at all in the operation! The Brahmin was convinced of Nanda's greatness and sent him to Chidambaram after having begged him to forgive him and to bless him with the knowledge of God. At Chidambaram Nanda passed through fire to get purified of his low birth as a pariah and merged in Nataraja as a mass of brilliant light!

There is a curious custom that a kind of preparation called *kali* is to be prepared to propitiate Nataraja on this occasion. The myth deriving the origin of the custom is as follows:

Once there lived a great devotee of Nataraja named Sendanar. The king, not recognising his greatness, had him imprisoned. His wife and son were eking out their livelihood by begging. One day the lad came to his mother in tears since he was insulted by his companions who taunted that he had no legitimate father. The woman approached her husband's teacher and master, one famous Pattinathar, at whose prayer, the elephant-headed deity Vināyaka restored Sendanar to his wife in a miraculous manner.

Sendanar was then directed to go to Chidambaram, earn money by selling twigs for fuel, and to feed one devotee of Śiva everyday with the money obtained thus.

He did this for a long time, but on account of incessant heavy rain, his fuel used to be wet and so could not command any buyer who would pay cash for it. Undaunted, he exchanged his bundle of twigs for a quantity of flour on the Arudra day, prepared this simple preparation called kali and offered it to Nataraja. Before partaking of it, he searched and also waited for a devotee of Śiva, who would partake of it first. Lord Nataraja himself is said to have partaken of the preparation, in the guise of an aged Brahmin, and disappeared with a quantity of it which was subsequently found strewn in his temple to be picked up and eaten by the people! The custom of preparing kali on the Arudra day is said to have originated from this incident.

Although this festival is observed in all places considered sacred for the worship of Śiva, yet Chidambaram in the South Arcot district is said to be specially important.

The other places held sacred for the worship of Nataraja and for the observance of the Arudra festival are Perur near Coimbatore, Kuttalam[2] near Tenkasi, Tinnevelly,[3] Madurai[4] and Tiruvalangadu near Madras (Chennai).

At Tiruvorriyur near Madras, in the temple of Audipurisvara, there are a number of lithic records, relating to gifts for the observance of the festival. On the south wall of the central shrine, there is a record of king Rajendrachola I (A.D. 1012-43), for bathing the god Mahadeva of that place with clarified butter on the birthday festival of the king which fell on the

Nakshatra Tiruvadirai in the month of Margali. Again, there is another of the 8th year of king Rajarajadeva making a gift of money for offerings to the god Karanai Vitankadeva, on the day of Tiruvadirai in the month of Margali.

On the north wall of the first prakara of the Arunajatesvara temple at Tirruppanandal[5] near Kumbakonam, there is a record of a Vijianagara king gifting land for conducting the festival of Margali Tiruvadirai.

The south wall of the mandapa in front of the Virattanesvara temple at Valvaur[6] near Mayavaram contains a record of the 5th year of the Chola king Rajadhirajadeva (1st July, 1167) gifting money for getting the *Tiruvembavai* recited before the image of Vadavurali Nayanar on Margali Tiruvadirai festival day.

On the north wall of the central shrine in the Karkotakesvara temple at Kamarasavalli,[7] Trichinopoly district, there is an inscription dated in the reign of Chola king Rajendrachola, 29th year, Risabha, Wednesday, Arudra, corresponding to May 6th, 1041 A.D., for performing the *Sakkai Kuttu* dance, thrice on each of the festivals Margali Tiruvadirai and Vaigasi Tiruvadirai.

On the west wall of the central shrine in the Mahalingasvaran temple at Tiruvidaimaruthur,[8] there is a record relating to the 37th year of king Parantaka I making gift of land for celebrating the Tiruvadirai festival.

On the western wall of the Nagesvarasvarin temple in Sulurpeta,[9] Nellore district, there is a record dated in the 2nd year of the reign of king Vijiayaganda-gopaladeva, about his giving land for the performance of a festival during Tiruvadirai.

NOTES

1 For details see *South Indian Shrines* by P.V. Jagadisa Ayyar.

2 This place is fully dealt with in Chapter XXXI of *South Indian Shrines* by P.V. Jagadisa Ayyar.

3 This place is fully dealt with in Chapter XXIX of *South Indian Shrines* by P.V. Jagadisa Ayyar.

4 These are numbered as 104 and 109 of 1912 in the record of *Madras Epigraphical Department* (Annual Reports published by the Government of Madras).

5 These are numbered as 42 of 1914 in the record of *Madras Epigraphical Department* (Annual Reports published by the Government of Madras).

6 These are numbered as 421 of 1912 in the record of *Madras Epigraphical Department* (Annual Reports published by the Government of Madras)

7 These are numbered as 65 of 1914 in the record of *Madras Epigraphical Department* (Annual Reports published by the Government of Madras)

8 These are numbered as 222 of 1907 in the record of *Madras Epigraphical Department* (Annual Reports published by the Government of Madras)

9 This is item No. 633 on page 1136 Vol. II of *Inscriptions of the Madras Presidency*, Government of Madras, 1919

XXVII   Vaikuntha Ekādaśi

The famous Vaikuntha Ekādaśi day of the Hindus is said to be the eleventh day of the bright fortnight in the month of Margasira or Margali, corresponding to the English months of December-January. The occasion also goes by the names, Mokshada Ekādaśi, or Ekādaśi that could secure for the observer of the Vrata, freedom from birth and death and liberation from bondage and Mukkodi Ekādaśi, or Ekādaśi equal in potency to innumerable ordinary Ekādaśi occasions put together.

The observance of the Vrata consists in rigid fasting followed by the worship of Vishṇu, one of the Hindu Trinity representing the preservative aspect in the universe. It is believed to have the effect of conferring on the observer long life, happiness and physical strength.

The origin of the names Vaikuntha Ekādaśi and Mukkodi Ekādaśi and the importance attached to the occasion are attributed to the incidents recorded in the following tradition:

In the bygone Krita age, called the golden age, there existed an asura named Muran in the city of Chandravati, who was harassing the devas and giving them a good deal of trouble. To get rid of him, and his troubles, the devas approached Vishṇu reposing on the back of a hydra in the ocean of milk, and made representations. Vishṇu thereupon is said to have condescended to descend on this mortal earth as an avatara or incarnation and destroy the asura. As his incarnation and the destruction of the asura are said to have taken place on an Ekādaśi day, and as he had descended from his abode in Vaikuntha, a region of bliss in the universe, the day came to be known as Vaikuntha Ekādaśi day.

The derivation of the name Ekādaśi is allegorical and interesting. Vishṇu is said to have fallen into a swoon while about to fight with the asuras, and a damsel of exquisite beauty is said to have arisen out of his body and destroyed the asuras for him. This damsel was subsequently named 'Ekādaśi' and the observers of the Ekādaśi Vrata are said to be blessed by this divine-born damsel.

The expression 'Mukkodi' is said to have originated from the fact that three crores of devas came into this mortal world with Vishṇu when he took incarnation to destroy the asuras.

There is an interesting allegorical myth of deep significance, emphasising the importance of the observance of Ekādaśi Vrata in general, and Vaikuntha Ekādaśi in particular. It is, in brief, as follows:

Once upon a time, there ruled over this earth a king named Rukmangadha. He had a fine Nanda Vana or flower garden where bloomed all sorts of fine, beautiful and rare flowers. Indra, the god of the celestials, was worshipping the Almighty deity and was in sore need for flowers for doing it properly. He came to know of Rukmangadha's garden. So he deputed some of his devas to procure enough flowers for him from there, and they were duly executing his orders for a long time. King Rukmangadha, though he missed the flowers from his garden every day, could not find out the thieves who stole them, since devas were invisible to mortals, and the flowers, as we know, were being taken daily by the devas.

The king's gardeners, zealous in the discharge of their duty, were carefully watching for any intruder on whom the charge of theft of the garden flowers might be laid.

One day, a sage named Jabali of great yogic power and merit, having selected a portion of Rukmangadha's flower garden, was meditating upon the one supreme intelligence pervading the universe, completely oblivious to all external world. The gardeners took him for a thief, disturbed him in his meditations and brought him before the king, after having accused him of theft of the flowers from the royal garden.

The king coming to know of Jabali's greatness and the folly of his menials in having given offence to the mighty sage, approached him with great reverence, and begged to be forgiven for the wrongs inflicted on the holy personage. The sage, an embodiment of patience, mercy and forgiveness, not only pardoned the king, but also gave him certain herbs, which when burnt in the royal flower garden, would reveal to him the mystery of the theft of flowers.

The deva minions of Indra, when they came to the royal gardens to gather flowers for their master's worship as usual, were materialised by the virtue of the plant burnt there by the orders of the king and became visible to ordinary mortals. They disclosed to the king their mission which resulted in the daily disappearance of flowers from his garden and as they were unable to ascend to their abode, the heavens, on account of the gross material particles clinging to their ethereal body of light and making it heavy, had to utilise the merit a washer woman had obtained by the observance of this Ekādaśi Vrata.

The story is of course allegorical and is meant to show that the clogging sensation of material existence, due to gross particles gathering around the jivas, or egos, may be made to disappear by the observance of the Vrata, which could shake off the grosser particles by the intensity of the vibrations, resulting in quietude, physical, emotional and mental. Though all temples dedicated to Vishnu are important for the observance of this Vrata, yet the Ranganatha temple at Srirangam[1] in Trichinopoly district is considered specially important.

On the rock to the west of the boulder known as Nagargundu, west of the steps leading to the Ardranarisvara temple on the hill at Tiruchchengodu,[2] Salem district, there is a record referring to the Chola king Rajakesarivarman making gifts of gold for feeding 20 Brahmins on the Ekādaśi day in the 13th year of his reign.

NOTES

1　This place is fully dealt with in Chapter XXVI of *South Indian Shrines* by P.V. Jagadisa Ayyar.
2　This is numbered as 629 of 1905 in the records of the *Madras Epigraphical Department* (Annual Reports published by the Government of Madras)

APPENDICES

Appendix I

The following table* shows the current names of the divisions of time in the different languages.

Language	60=	60=	7=	2=	2=	6=	2=	
English	Indian minute	Indian hour	Day	Week	Fortnight	Month	Half-year	Year
Sanskrit	Vinaudy	Naudy	Dinam	Vauram	Paksham	Mausam	Ayanam	Samvatsaram
Tamil	Vinaudy	Nauzhiga	Naul	Vauram	Paksham	Mausam	Ayanam	Varsham
Telugu	Vighadiya	Ghadiya	Dinam	Vauram	Paksham	Tingal	Ayanam	Samvatsaram
Canarese	Vighaligey	Ghaligey	Dinam	Vauram	Paksham	Tingal	Ayanam	Varsham
Malayalam	Vinaudicay	Nauzhiga	Divasam	Autchavattam	Paksham	Mausam	Ayanam	Varsham

* Extract from page 143 of *Manual of the Administration of the Madras Presidency*, Vol.III, Government of Madras, 1893.

Appendix II

The following table* shows the signs of the fixed sidereal zodiac displayed against lunar mansions.

No.	Hindu Name		European Name		Dravidian Solar month	Approximate beginning of English month	Remarks
1	Mesham	(ram)	Aries	(ram)	Chitrai	April 12th	
2	Rishabham	(bull)	Tauras	(bull)	Vaikhasi	May 13th	
3	Mithunam	(twins)	Gemini	(twins)	Auni	June 13th	
4	Karkatakam	(crab)	Cancer	(crab)	Audi	July 15th	
5	Simham	(lion)	Leo	(lion)	Auvani	August 15th	
6	Kanni	(virgin)	Virgo	(virgin)	Purattasi	September 15th	
7	Tulam	(balance)	Libra	(balance)	Aippasi	October 16th	
8	Vrichikham	(scorpion)	Scorpio	(scorpion)	Kartigai	November 15th	
9	Dhanu	(bow)	Sagittarius	(archer)	Margali	December 14th	
10	Makaram	(alligator)	Capricornus	(goat)	Tai	January 12th	
11	Kumbham	(pot)	Aquarius	(water-man)	Masi	February 12th	
12	Meenam	(fish)	Pisces	(fish)	Panguni	March 12th	

* Extract from page 754 of *Manual of the Administration of the Madras Presidency*, Vol.III, Government of Madras, 1893

Appendix III

The following* are the different vernacular names for the points of the compass with their presiding deities in the Hindu system according to the Hindu *Sastras*.

No.	English	Sanskrit	Tamil	Telugu	Canarese	Malayalam	Presiding deities (Ashta-dikpalakas)	Elephants of the quarters (Ashta-dikgajams)
1	North	Uttiram	Vadak	Uttiram	Vadagu	Vadak	Kubera	Saurabuman
2	North-east	Esanyam	Vada-kizak	Esanyam	Esanyam	Vada-kizak	Esana	Supradeepam
3	East	Poorvam	Kizak	Toorp	Moodloo	Kizak	Indra	Airavatam
4	South-east	Agneyam	Ten-kizak	Agneyam	Temmoodloo	Tek-kizak	Agni	Pundareekam
5	South	Dakshinam	Terkku	Dakshinam	Tenka	Tek	Yama	Vaumanam
6	South-west	Neirritam	Ten-merk	Neirritam	Tempadoov aloo	Tek-padinyaur	Nirriti	Kumudam
7	West	Paśchimam	Merk	Pademara	Padoovaloo	Padinyaur	Varuṇa	Anjanam
8	North-west	Vauyavyam	Vadamerk	Vauyavyam	Vauyavyam	Vadak-padinyaur	Vāyu	Pushpadantam

*Extract from page 902 of *Manual of the Administration of the Madras Presidency*, Vol.III, Government of Madras, 1893

Appendix IV

The twenty-seven* *Nakshattras* or Asterisms (constellations) are:

1. Aśvini — *Beta* Arietis (Asvinau — 3 stars).
2. Bharani — 35 Arietis or Musca (Yamah — 3 stars).
3. Krittika — *Pi* Tauri or Pleiades (Agnih — 6 stars).
4. Rohini — *Alpha* Tauri or Aldebaran (Prajapatih — 5 stars).
5. Mrigasira — *Lambda* Orionis (Somah — 3 stars).
6. Ardra — *Alpha* Orionis (Rudrah — 1 star).
7. Punarvasu — *Beta* Geminornum or Pollux (Aditih — 5 or 4 stars).
8. Pushya — *Delta* Cancri (Brihaspatih — 3 or 7 stars).
9. Aslesha — *Epsilon* Hydrae (Sarpah — 6 or 5 stars).
10. Māgha — *Alpha* Leonis Regulus (Pitarah — 5 or 4 stars).
11. Purva-Phalguni — *Delta* Leonis (Bhagah — 2 stars).
12. uttara-Phalguni — *Beta* Leonis (Aryama — 2 stars).
13. Hasta — *Delta* Corvi (Savita — 5 stars).
14. Chittra — *Alpha* Virginis or Spica (Tvashta — 1 or 6 stars).
15. Svāti — *Alpha* Bootes or Arcturus (Vayuh - 1 star).
16. Vaiśākha — *Lota* Librae (Indragni — 5 or 4 stars).
17. Anuradha — *Delta* Scorpionis (Mitrah — 3 or 4 stars).
18. Jyeshtha — *Alpha* Scorpionis or Antares (Indrah — 3 stars).
19. Mula — *Lambda* Scorpionis (Nirritoh — 5 or 11 stars).
20. Purvashadha — *Delta* Sagittarii (Apah — 2 or 4 stars).
21. Uttarashadha — *Sigma* Sagittarii (Visvedevah — 4 stars).
22. Śravana — *Alpha* Aquilae or Al-tair (Vishnuh — 3 stars).
23. Dhanishtha — *Beta* Delphini (Vasavah — 3 or 4 stars).
24. Satabhisha — *Lambda* Aquarii (Varunah — 3 or 100 stars).
25. Purva-Bhādrapada — *Alpha* Pegasi (Aja Ekapad — 2 stars).
26. Uttara-Bhādrapada — *Gamma* Pegasi or Andromedae (Ahirbudhnyah — 2 stars).
27. Revati — *Zeta* Piscium (Pusha — 3 or 32 stars).

---

* Pages 211 and 212 *Age of Sankara*, T.S. Narayana Sastri, 1918.

Appendix V

*Comparison between the deities of the Brahmanical system and those of Roman and Egyptian systems. The following table will show the general correspondence between the principal Hindu deities of southern India and those of Rome and Egypt. The worship of Osiris and Isis more especially is nearly related, in its essential points, to the worship of Śiva and his consort Bhawani or Parvati.

Indian	Roman	Egyptian
Śiva	Jupiter	Osiris
Durga	Ceres	Isis
Bhagavatee	Venus	Isis
Bhawani or Parvati	Juno	Isis
Kāli	Proserpine	Isis
Annapurna	Ceres	Isis
Gaṇesh	Janus	Isis
Nandy	Minotaurus	Apis
Vishṇu	Jupiter	Osiris
Lakshmi	Venus	Isis
Krishṇa	Apollo	Osiris
Brahmā	Jupiter	Osiris
Surya	Apollo	Horus
Kubera	Plutus	Horus
Kārtikeya	Mars	Papremis
Yama	Pluto	Serapis
Indra	Jupiter tonans	Osiris
Viśwakarma	Vulcan	Thoth
Budha	Neptune	Osiris
Ganga	Styx	Nile
Menoo	Minos	Menes
Narada	Mercury	Apis

---

* Footnote 26 on page 79 of *Manual of the Administration of the Madras Presidency.* Vol. III., Government of Madras, 1893, Vol.I.

* The following list is taken from 'Prinsep's Useful Tables' published in 1834.

1. The Infinite Almighty Creator of the Vedas, Brahm.

The Hindu Trinity, or Trimurti:	Brahma,	Vishnu,	Śiva.
Their consorts:	Saraswati,	Lakshmi,	Parvati,
	Śakti or Maya,	Padma or Sri,	Bhawani or Durga.
Their attributes:	Creator,	Preserver,	Destroyer.
Their attendant vāhana or vehicle:	Hamsa (goose),	Garuda (bird),	Nandi (bull).
Their symbols:	Times, Air,	Water,	Fire.
Their stations:	Meru,	The Sun,	Jupiter.
Their common titles, A.U.M.	Parameśwara,	Nārāyana,	Mahādeva.
Figure under which worshipped:	Mentally,	Saligram and 9 avataras	The lingam, under his million epithets
Analogues in Western mythology:	Saturn,	Jupiter,	Jupiter.

2. Other members of the Hindu pantheon, and their supposed analogues in Western mythology, according to Sir. Wm. Jones.

Saraswati.	Minerva, patroness of learning.
Ganesha.	Janus, god of wisdom.
Indra.	Jupiter, god of firmament.
Varuna.	Neptune, god of water.
Prithvi.	Cybele, goddess of earth.
Viśwakarma.	Vulcan, architect of gods.

---

* Pages 76 and 77 of *Faiths, Fairs and Festivals of India*, Buck. Thacker, Spink & Co., Calcutta, 1917.

Kārtikeya or Skanda.	Mars, god of war.
Kāma.	Cupid, god of love.
Surya, or Arka.	Sol, the sun, Mithra, the same.
Hanuman, son of Pavana.	Pan, the monkey-god
Rama.	Bacchus, god of wine.
Yama.	Pluto or Minos.
Heracula.	Hercules.
Aswiculapa.	Aesculapius (genii).
Vaitarini.	The river Styx.
Durga.	Juno.
Narada.	Mercury, music.
Krishṇa.	Apollo.
Bhawani.	Venus.
Kāli or Durga	Proserpine.
Agni.	Vulcan, Fire.
Swaha.	Vesta (his wife).
Aświni Kumara.	Castor and Pollux.
Aruna.	Aurora.
Atavi Devi.	Diana.
Kubera.	Plutus, god of riches.
Ganga.	The river Ganges.
Vāyu.	Aeolus.
Sri.	Ceres.
Annapurna.	Anna Parenna.

* The gods and goddesses of Greece are but copies of their Hindu originals.

Jupiter	Stands for	Indra.
Juno	Stands for	Durga or Parvati (Indrani.)
Apollo	Stands for	Krishṇa
Venus	Stands for	Rati

---

* Page 407 and 408 *Hindu Superiority*, Sarda, 1917.

Ceres	Stands for	Sri
Cybele	Stands for	Prithvi
Neptune and Uranu	Stand for	Varuṇa
Minerva	Stands for	Saraswati
Mars	Stands for	Skand
Pluto	Stands for	Yama
Plutus	Stands for	Kubera
Vulcan	Stands for	Viśwakarma
Cupid	Stands for	Kāma
Mercury	Stands for	Narada
Aurora	Stands for	Ushas
Aeolus	Stands for	Vāyu
Janus	Stands for	Gaṇesha
Dioscuri (Castor and Pollux.)	Stand for	Aswini Kumara
Styx	Stands for	Vaitarni
Ida	Stands for	Kailash
Olympus	Stands for	Meru

Appendix VI

* The *Rupamandana* gives a summary of the description of the colours, weapons and emblems and vehicles and seats of the nine *grahas,* which may be tabularly presented thus:-

Name of the deity	Weapons etc.			Seat amd vehicle	Remarks
	Colour	Right-hand.	Left-hand		
Surya.	White	Padma	Padma	Chariot with seven horses.	*All the nine deities should be adorned with kirita and ratna-kundalas*
Soma.	White	Kumud	Kumuda	Chariot with ten horses.	
Bhauma.	Red	Danda	Kamandala	A goat	
Budha.	Yellow	Hands in	Yogamudra	Sarpasana	
Guru.	Yellow	Akshamala	Kamandalu	Hamsa	
Śukra.	White	Akshamala	Kamandalu	A frog	
Śani.	Black	Danda	Kamandalu		
Rāhu.	Smoke-colour			A sacrificial pit (*kunda*).	
Ketu.	Smoke-colour	Arms folded as in the *anjali* attitude.		The lower portion of the body of Rāhu should be that of a snake.	

*   Pages 322 and 323 Elements of Hindu Iconography, T.A. Gopinatha Rao, Law Printing House, Madras, 1914 and 1916, Vol.I, Part I.

Appendix VII
* NARRATIVES ABOUT PLANETS.

Departments	Sun	Moon	Mars	Mercury	Jupiter	Venus	Saturn
Color	Copper	White	Red	Green	Yellow	Mixed(Gold & Silver)	Black
Nature	Satwa	Satwa	Tamas	Rajas	Satwa	Rajas	Tamas
Sex	Male	Female	Male	Eunuch (Female)	Male	Female	Eunuch (Male)
Caste	Kshatriya	Vaisya	Kshatriya	Sudra	Brahmin	Brahmin	Chandala
Elements	Fire	Water	Fire	Earth	Ether	Water	Air
Deities	Agni	Varuna	Subrahmanya	Vishnu	Indra	Indrani	Brahmā
Garments	Thick	New	Half-burnt	Wet	Shabby	Strong	Rag
Metals	Copper	Gems	Gold	Brass	Silver	Pearls	Iron (lead)
Parts	Bones	Blood	Marrow	Skin	Flesh & brain	Semen	Muscles
Grains	Wheat	Paddy	Lentil	Greengram	Bengalgram	Beans	Sesame
Seasons	Summer	Winter	Summer	Autumn	Snow	Spring	All seasons
Taste	Pungent	Salt	Acerbity	Mixed	Sweet& cool	Sour	Bitter & Astringent
Residence	Place of worship	Springs	Fire	Playground	Storehouse	Bed-chamber	Dustbin
Temperament	Bilious	Phlegmatic	Bilious	Mixed	Phlegmatic	Windy & Phlegmatic	Windy

* Page 248 of *Kalaprakssika*, N.P. Subramania Ayyar, 1917.

Appendix VIII

*INTRODUCTION TO HINDU FESTIVALS.
*(From Wilson's *Essays on the Religion of the Hindus*, Vol. II,. p. 151).

"Among all the nations of the ancient world a considerable portion of the year was devoted to the solemnization of public festivals, at which the people found in the assemblage of multitudes, in the exhibition of games, and in religious pageants and ceremonies, a compensation for the want of those more refined entertainments which are created by the necessities and the luxury of a more advanced stage of civilization. Some of these primitive celebrations have retained their hold upon national tastes and feelings long after their origin and meaning were forgotten, and become interwoven with new conditions of society, with altered manners and institutions, and with a total change of religion. In all the countries of Europe they have left at least traces of their former prevalence in the nomenclature of our calendars, and many of the holidays which are appropriated to the saints of the Christian Church have been borrowed from the public festivals of ancient paganism. In proportion also as nations, or as different classes of the same nation, retain their primitive habits, the observances of olden times enjoy their veneration, and interest their affections. They are, however, fast fading in the Western world, even from the faith of tradition, before the extension of knowledge and refinement, and before the augmented demands for toil which the present artificial

---

* Page 1 to 5 of *Hindu and Mahammadan Festivals*, John Murdoch, 1904.

modes of life impose, when holidays are denounced as an unprofitable interruption of productive industry, and a festival or a fair is condemned as a wasteful expenditure of time and money. It is only, therefore, in regions remote from the reach of the taskmaster, where exemption from work is occasionally the equal right of all classes of the community, that we may expect to find the red letters of the calendar significant signs — importing what they designate — public holidays — days on which the artificer and the peasant rest from physical exertion, and spend some passing hours in a kindly communion of idleness with their fellows, in which, if the plough stands still and anvil is silent, the spirit of social intercourse is kept alive, and man is allowed to feel that he was born for some nobler end than to earn the scanty bread of the pauper by the unrelaxing labour of the slave.

It is in the remote East, and especially in India, that we may expect to find the living representation of ancient observances, and the still existing solemnizations which delighted the nations of antiquity, and we shall not be altogether disappointed; although even here they begin to languish under the influence of a foreign government, under the unsympathizing superiority which looks upon the enjoyments of a different race with disdain, under the prevalence of the doctrine which regards public holidays as deductions from public wealth, and under the principles of a system of religious faith which, although it might be indulgent to popular recreations, cannot withhold its disapprobation of them when their objects and origin are connected with falsehood and superstition. From the operation of these causes, the Hindu festivals have already diminished both in frequency and in attraction; and they may become, in the course of time, as little familiar to the people of India as those of European institution are to the nations of the West. They will then, perhaps, become also objects of curiosity and interest; and in anticipation of that period, and in order to secure an account of them whilst it is still possible to learn what they are, I propose to offer to the Society some notices of the religious Fasti of the Hindus and calendar of their public festivals.

The different celebrations of the Hindus are specified in their almanacs and are described at length in different works, such as the Tithi Tattwa, Tithi Kritya, Vratarka, Kala Nirnaya, the Kalpa Druma of Jaya Sinha, and others, and also in passages of several of the Puranas, particularly in the Bhavishyottara, which, as it usually occurs, treats exclusively of the festivals. The observances are, for the most part, the same in the different provinces of India, but there are some peculiar to peculiar localities; and even those which are universally held, enjoy various degrees of popularity in different places, and are celebrated with various local modifications. The periods also vary within certain limits, according as the lunar month is reckoned to begin from the new moon, or from the full moon; the former mode of computation prevailing in Bengal and in Telingana, whilst in Hindustan and in the Tamil countries of the South the latter is followed.* My opportunities of personal observation have been in a great degree limited to Bengal, and for the rest of India I can speak but imperfectly of any existing practices which may not exactly conform to those enjoined by original works, or of which no account has been published by actual observer. One object of communicating these notices to the Society is, therefore, the supplying of this deficiency.

---

* [Prinsep's useful Tables, ed. E. Thomas, p. 154 f.]

Amongst the Members of the Society* are many who, in the course of their public services, must have witnessed the celebration of the Hindu festivals in different and distant places: their better knowledge will enable them to furnish correct information respecting those local peculiarities with which I am unacquainted; and I hope that they may be induced to favour the Society with the results of their experience, and contribute to render the description of the popular festivals of the Hindus as complete and authentic as those who may take an interest in the topic have a right to expect from us.

Upon the examining the Fasti of the nations of antiquity, it is obvious that many of their festivals originated either from the same or similar motives. They all bear a religious character, inasmuch as religious worship formed part of the celebration; but that was the spirit of the time. However erroneously directed, the feelings of the multitude in the heathen world associated the powers of heaven, real or imaginary, with all their transactions but the sources to which I more especially refer, however closely linked with this common sentiment, are in some degree varieties of it: they constitute the species, and are obviously reducible to two principal distinctions, which may be regarded as universal or particular. The universal festivals which are probably traceable among all nations elevated above barbarism, and which may have been handed down by tradition from the earliest periods in the history of the human race, are manifestly astronomical, and are intended to commemorate the revolutions of the planets, the alterations of the seasons, and the recurrence of cyclical intervals of longer or shorter

---

* The Bengal Royal Asiatic Society, in whose Journal the account first appeared, 1849. Vol. IX. pp. 10-110.

duration. The particular festivals are those arising out of national forms of religious worship, out of the different mythological creations of priests or poets, or out of imperfect narratives, transmitted orally through succeeding generations, of occurences anterior to historical record. In as far as these traditions may have related to the great mass of mankind, before it was broken up into detached communities, or as the mythological fictions may typify real personages or events of the same era, or may embody objects, likely to be presented to the imaginations of men under similar aspects, we need not be surprised to meet with analogies of deep interest, even in the festivals which are of particular institution. It is, however, in those which relate to the course of time and the phenomena of the planetary sphere that anologies are most likely to occur, and do, in fact, present themselves in the practices of distant and apparently unconnected races.

The coincidences that may be discovered between the universal or particular festivals of the various nations of antiquity, form a subject that well deserves careful and patient investigation. It would, in all probability, tend to confirm the remarkable results which comparative philology has of late so unanswerably demonstrated, and furnish corroborative testimony of the relationship of races, which, however dissimilar now, in physical configuration, social condition, and national character, are proved to be of kindred origin by the unequivocal affinities of language. In like manner as the Greek, Latin, Teutonic, Celtic, Slavonic, and Sanskrit tongues have been shown to be allied by principles common to them all, so in all probability it would be found that the festivals and holidays which once animated the cities of Athens and Rome, the forests of Germany and the steppes of Russia, are still continuing to afford seasons of public recreation to the dark complexioned tribes that people the borders of the Indus and the Ganges. The full development of these identifications is, however, a work of time and of research exceeding what I can bestow upon it; and I must be content with contributing only that portion of the materials requisite for its investigation which relates to the Fasti of the Hindus, briefly suggesting, as I proceed, one or two of the most obvious points of apparent similarity.

The subject of the festivals of the Hindu year was introduced to the Asiatic Society of Bengal by Sir William Jones, who published a paper on it in the third volume of the Researches. What he thought of the inquiry is evident from the manner in which he speaks of the authority whence his information was derived, and which he calls a wonderfully curious tract of the learned and celebrated Raghunandana. It was no doubt this Tithi Tattwa, a standard text-book, as are all the works of the same author, in Bengal. Sir William Jones, however, has taken from this work only the heads of the descriptions, and omits all the particulars into which it enters, with the exceptions of a few brief notes; and his details are neither sufficiently full nor interesting to inspire others with the sentiments with which he contemplated the subject. Some years ago I collected materials for its fuller elucidation, and published in one of the Calcutta papers brief notices of the festivals as they occurred; but the notices were merely popular, and were necessarily short and unconnected, and they have never been presented in a collective form. The topic is one, therefore, which, if destitute of other recommendation, possesses, even in these latter days, that of some degree of novelty, and may on this account be further acceptable to the Society.

As remarked by Sir William Jones, although most of the Indian fasts and festivals are regulated by the days of the moon, yet the most solemn and remarkable of them have a manifest reference to the supposed motions of the sun. An attempt is usually made to adjust the one to the other; but the principles on which the adjustment of the solar to the lunar year is based, are of a somewhat complicated character, and are not essential to a knowledge of the periods at which the festivals are held, and which, with a few exceptions, are sufficiently determinate."

Appendix IX

SKETCH* ACCOUNT OF THE PRINCIPAL HINDU RELIGIOUS
FESTIVALS OF SOUTHERN INIDA—

Introduction — Besides the feasts peculiar to each district
and temple, which return several times in the course of a year,
the Hindus have many more, which are held only once a year,
and are commonly observed through the whole country. The
religious festivals are closely connected with the systems of
astronomy and chronology by which their periods are
determined. The pure Tamil festivals follow the solar
computation, and happen on the same day each year; unless
there is a variation of one day on account of minor
astronomical disturbances. The only representatives of this
class at the present day are Pongal in the winter, the Tamil
New-year in the spring, and the Audipundigay in mid-year.
The rest are all reckoned by lunar time (like the English
Easter), and fall at different dates each year; and as these
calculations depend upon the particular data and mode of
reckoning that may be adopted, the times of certain festivals
differ slightly even in the same year in various parts of the
country, in the same way that Easter is kept at different dates
in the same year by the members of the Greek and Latin
churches. Hence the high estimation in which almanacs are
held by the Hindus.

A description of each of the principal festivals is given
below beginning with the Telugu new year:-

(2) *Telugu New Year.* — This falls at the end of March or
beginning of April. It is also the first day of the year for

---

* Footnote 34 on pp. 92 to 94 of Manual of the Administration of the
Madras Presidency. Vol.III, Government of Madras, 1893, Vol. I.

Canarese and Mahrattas, but not for Tamils. Three days' rejoicing takes place, with exhibitions of fireworks and discharging 8 guns. Early in the morning each person anoints his body with oil and bathes in warm water. In the evening the family priest reads out passages from the new almanac, the family listening to hear their fortune during the coming year.

(3) *Shree Ramanavami.* — This is the birthday of Rama, an incarnation of Vishnu. It is observed chiefly by Mahratta Vaishnavites, but also to some extent by the Canarese and Telugus. It is not a Dravidian festival, and was introduced into the country by the Mahrattas. It occurs on the ninth day of the month Chaitra, or about the end of March. The image of the hero is set up, adorned, and worshipped; and portions of the Ramayana, or poetical history of Rama, his romantic adventures in search of his wife, and his success in rescuing her from the giants who had carried her off, are sung to large audiences. Festivals are also observed in Vishnu temples, especially in the shrines dedicated to Rama, for ten days ending with the birthday. In the Tamil countries, the birthday is observed in the Tamil month of Chaitra, which is a month later.

(4) *Mylapore Ratotsavam.* — This is a local car festival. It takes place about the seventh day of Pungoony, that is to say, in March or April. It is held in honour of the God Kapauleshwara, and lasts for ten days. The car procession takes place on the seventh day.

(5) *Mylapore Aroopatmoovar.* — This falls on the day after the last.

Sixty-three saints are taken in procession.

(6) *Pungoony Oottiram.* — This takes place in the month of Pungoony, that is to say, in March or April. It lasts for fifteen days. Its origin is in the following tale. Siva was

conducting the united offices of the Trinity — creating, preserving, and destroying. His consort, Parvati, went behind her husband and put her hands over his eyes, the result being that the whole world was enveloped in darkness. Siva thereupon cursed her and deposed her from her position of wife. Afterwards regretting what he had done, but being unable to restore her, he instructed her to sit for six months in the Kumbanuddy tank in Yecambaran temple and meditate on the deity, at the end of which time he appeared before her and restored to her her privileges. This is symbolized on the tenth day of the feast by placing images of the god and goddess (*Kaumatchy*) together in one chamber. At Conjeeveram at the wedding hour of the deities, private marriages are performed within the precincts of the temple.

(7) *Tamil New Year.* — This falls on April 12th, the first day of the Tamil month Chitra. It is observed in the same way as the Telugu new year; but no anointment takes place, the day being dedicated on the part of the Brahmins to the spirits of departed ancestors.

(8) *Narsimha Jayanti.* — In honour of the lion-man, the fourth incarnation of Vishnu, in which he destroyed the giant Hiranyacasip. On this day Vaishnavas fast till the evening, when after worshipping the god, they eat in company. The special offering to Narsimha is sugar-water (*paunacam*). This festival falls on the 13th day of the second month Vaishakha.

(9) *Garooda Ootsavam at Triplicane.* — This occurs on the third day of the month Chitra, that is to say, in April or May. It is held in honour of the God Parthasarathy at the place named.

(10) *Ratotsavam at Triplicane.* — This is a car festival and is held in conjunction with the last, occurring four days later, that is to say, on the seventh day of Chitra.

(11) *Garooda Ootsavam at Conjeeveram.* — This takes place in the month of Vaiyasy, or in May. It lasts ten days, during each of which the Vishnu idol Varadarajaswami visits Siva Canjy, or Larger Canjy, on various *vahanas* for the purpose of permitting the other deities to pay their respects to him. He thus goes down the street two miles long, which leads from his own temple to the Rajaveethy, at the foot of which he rests for a while in a mantapam belonging to him. Varadaraja and Yecambaranathar, the Siva idol, are held to be brothers-in-law, and the evening of the sixth day of the feast is occupied by a visit to the Siva temple. The image is brought down to the front of it, taken thrice round about from right to left and the same number of times the opposite way, and then taken away again. This festival is a display of Vaishnavism against the old Shaivism.

(12) *Auny Amavasya.* — This is the new moon festival of the month of Auny. The floating festival at Trivellore falls on this date.

(13) *Audy Amavasya.* — This is the new moon occurring in the solar month Audy, and is observed only by the Tamils.

(14) *Auvanimoolum.* — This is held in the month of Auvany, that is to say, in August or September, on the day on which the constellation *Moolam* appears. It is observed only by the Tamils.

(15) *Vara Lakshmi Vratam.* — This occurs in the month of Audy, or about August. It is a festival attended by women only, who make offerings to Lakshmi, the wife of Vishnu, and invoke her aid in preserving them from being widows. Each woman celebrates the festival in her own house.

(16) *Avaniyavattam or Oopacarmam.* — This is peculiar to the three twice-born castes, and is the annual renewal of their sacred order, a new thread being put on. One meal only is taken on this day. It occurs generally in August.

(17) *Gocoola Ashtamy* and *Shree Jayanthy* or *Krishna Jananam.* — The birth-day of Krishna, an incarnation of Vishnu, which falls on the 7th or 8th day of the fifth month Shrauvana, or about the end of August. It is observed chiefly by Vaishnavas, and particularly by the class of cowherds who are denominated Yadavas. It is a fasting day for Brahmins. In the evening the sectarians bathe, and after worshipping Krishna by offerings of tulasi (*ocymum sanctum*) and other flowers parade in the streets with hilarity. Sweetmeats are manufactured on this occasion in great variety. On the evening of the following day the images are carried in procession. Cow-herds keep up special rejoicings.

(18) *Saumavaidy Oopacarmam.* — This is similar to the Oopacarmam mentioned above. It is however observed only by those of the three twice-born castes who belong to the Saumaveda school of philosophy.

(19) *Pillayar Chowthy* or *Vinayaka Chatoorty.* — This occurs on the fourth day of the sixth month Bhadrapada and is in honour of Vinayaka or Pillayar, son of Siva, who is worshipped by all Shaivites as the dispenser of learning and the remover of difficulties from suitable understandings. This deity is also called Vigneshwara and Ganesh. On the day in question clay images of the deity, riding upon the back of a rat, are made, duly consecrated, and worshipped in houses and families; they are afterwards thrown into a river or tank.

(20) *Ananta Chatoordashee.* — This is a religious ceremony observed by males only. It occurs on the 14th day of the sixth month. At the break of day the Brahmin family priest consecrates a vessel, by reciting certain formulas. He is then presented with cloths and money. This ceremony is performed only by those who have previously made a vow.

(21) *Mahalaya Amavasya.* — This is the new moon of the lunar month Bhadrapada, when ceremonies are performed in

honour of deceased ancestors, and food is offered to them. The whole fortnight indeed ending with the new moon is held sacred to the deceased ancestors, and goes under the name of *Mahalya Pacsham;* ceremonies being performed on the Tithi of the deceased by the surviving heir who performed his funeral obsequies.

(22) *Saraswatee Poojarambham — Ayudha Pujah* and *Dusserah.* This festival is principally in honour of deceased ancestors. It corresponds to the Durga Pujah of Bengal, and is supposed to commemorate a victory obtained by Durga, wife of Siva, over a demon. It is celebrated on the 7th, 8th and 10th days of the seventh month Ashwina, or in October, and is religiously kept. On this day the upper classes of Hindus make offerings of rice, fruit, flowers and new clothes to their ancestors. Brahmins worship Saraswati, the goddess of learning. Every one offers sacrifice also to the tools and implements which he uses in the exercise of his profession, the labourer to his plough, the mason to his trowel, women to their rice mill, & c. This ceremony is the Ayudha Pujah (sacrifice to implements). In former times princes gave public shows with a distribution of prizes on these occasions.

(23) *Deepavali* or the feast of lights. — This is celebrated on the 28th day of the seventh month, which occurs in October or November. The name means the feast of lamps, and a great number of lamps and lanterns are hung round the door of houses. Husbandmen offer sacrifices to the fields, and in some places to the dunghill. The chief observance at this festival is an oil-bath early in the morning, which is considered equivalent to bathing in the Ganges. Fire works and crackers are also used in large quantities and guns are fired. This feast is possibly a relic of ancient fire-worship.

(24) *Gowry.* — This is held on the third day of the sixth month Bhadrapada or in the beginning of September, and lasts

several days. It is principally in honour of Siva's wife Parvathy, one of whose names is Gowry. The festival is concluded by erecting a shapeless statue in each village, composed of paste of grain and intended to represent the Goddess. This image is finally placed under a canopy, and carried through the streets.

(25) *Bharani Deepam.* — This is a feast of lights celebrated in honour of Vishnu. It occurs in November or December.

(26) *Kartigay.* — A similar festival to the Deepavali, observed by Tamils only. It occurs on the full moon day in the solar month Kartigay when the constellation Kartigay appears. In some parts of the country most of the observances of the deepavaly are adopted at the Kartigay.

(27) *Vishnoo Deepam* or *Perumal Tirunal.* — In honour of Perumal or Vishnu celebrated by the Vaishnavas. It is generally celebrated on the day after Kartigay, and is considered to be the day on which Bulichakravarthy obtained immortality, he being the one of the seven *Chiranjeevis* or the undying who live till the end of the world.

(28) *Vaikunta Ekadasy.* — This occurs on the 11th day of the ninth month Margasheersha, or in December, and is a special festival of the Vaishnavas. On this day the gates of paradise are open to all pious people; hence another name for the feast, *viz.,* Swargadwara, 'gate of heaven.' It is a fasting day for both Brahmins and Shoodras. The feast is particularly sacred at Shreerangam, though common to Vishnu temples in general.

(29) *Aroodra Darsanam.* — This is held in the month of Margaly, that is to say, in December or January. It lasts for ten days. It is particularly sacred at Chidambaram.

(30) *Bhogy Pundigay.* — This is an unimportant festival except for the fact that it immediately precedes the Pongal and is generally looked upon as part of that feast. It occurs on the last day of the month of Margaly, or in January. There are no

particular religious ceremonies connected with this festival. It is looked upon as a period for relaxation.

(31) *Pongal* or *Sancranty.* — This is one of the most famous festivals. It is celebrated on the first day of the Hindu month Makara or Tai, which falls about the 11th or 12th of January, that being the day on which the sun passes from Saggitarius to Capricornus, and lasts three days, during which time the Tamilians employ themselves in visiting their friends. This feast is such for two reasons. The first that the month of Margaly (December), every day in which is unlucky, is about to expire; and the other, that it is to be succeeded by a month, each day of which is fortunate. In order to guard against evil, every morning during the month of December the women of the family scour a space before the door of each house, upon which are drawn by means of flour certain white lines. Upon these lines are placed balls of cow-dung, each bearing a citron blossom. The balls are daily picked up and preserved, and on the last day of the month, the women put the whole in a basket, and go with music to some waste place, where they deposit the relics. The meaning of these very primitive customs has yet to be examined. The first day of the succeeding festival is called Bhogy Pongal, and is kept by inviting near relations to an entertainment. The second day is called Surya (Sun) Pongal, or Peroom (great) Pongal, and is set apart in honour of the sun. Married women having purified themselves by bathing clothed, boil rice and milk in the open air. This is the chief day for visits. The second day is called the Pongal of cows. A mixture is made of water, saffron, and leaves, with which the cattle are sprinkled. The animals are then adorned with garlands, their horns are painted, and strings of coconuts and other fruits are hung on them. They are then driven out with music, and allowed to graze, for the rest of the day without a keeper. The festival concludes with a procession of idols to the village common.

(32) *Tai Amavasya.* — This is the new moon falling in the solar month Tai, and is observed only by Tamils. *Shraddha*, or funeral offerings to deceased ancestors, are performed specially on this day by the Hinduized upper classes; presents being at the same time made to Brahmins. The favourable days for this purpose are the new moons from August to January, but the Tai Amavasya is the chief.

(33) *Taipoosham.* — This day is sacred to Soobramaniya, the second son of Siva. The feast is particularly observed at the shrine of Pulney in Madura. The day is considered auspicious for purposes of education, next after the Dusserah. The harvest feast is observed on the same day in Vishnu temples.

(34) *Maha Shivaratri.* — "The night of Siva," a festival of great importance among Lingayets. It is celebrated on the 28th day of the Hindu month Magha, at the end of February or beginning of March, and the ceremonies consist of purification of the Lingas. After sacrifices, the celebrators should pass the night awake, employing themselves in reading *pooranas* relating to Siva. The feast is particularly observed at Kalastry in North Arcot district.

(35) *Maghizhady sevay* at Tiruvattore. — This occurs in the month Mausy, in February.

(36) *Holy Pundigay, Hootausana Powrnamy* or *Kaumanpandigay.* — Celebrated on the full moon of the lunar month Phalgoona, occurring generally in March. It is observed principally by the lower classes to commemorate the destruction of Kama (Cupid) by the God Siva. At the close of the festival a pile is lighted in every village, on which a cake is placed. In Bengal it is called Holy, or Swinging festival. In Travancore cocks are offered by Nayars, who kill them before the door of the temple of Kalee or Bhagavatee.